PROTECTED

REFLECTIONS OF A SECRET SERVICE AGENT

PROTECTED

REFLECTIONS OF A SECRET SERVICE AGENT

TIM VIERTEL

 LUCIDBOOKS

In memory of my parents,
Dr. Weldon and Joyce Viertel,
who served so faithfully and for so many years on
foreign mission fields around the world. Though they
served in seeming obscurity, their impact on the Kingdom
will be felt for years to come.

Table of Contents

Preface

DURING A 25-YEAR career with the Secret Service and seven years with Samaritan's Purse International Relief and the Billy Graham Evangelistic Association, God has allowed me to witness many things and experience countless adventures worldwide. These adventures have taken me from the poorest of war-torn countries to the seats of world power and the halls of the White House and Congress. From working around presidents, heads of state, and dignitaries, to conducting criminal investigations on the streets, this is the platform the Lord has given me, and I strive to use it for his glory.

Over the years, I have used many of the experiences in this book as illustrations when teaching adult and college Bible studies and speaking to church groups around the country. While I hope my audiences remembered the spiritual lessons in each story, I repeatedly got requests to put my experiences into print. Until recently, I never felt the urge to write such a book because it always seemed self-serving. I tend to be a little introverted and am usually happy not to call much attention to myself. However, as I started having grandchildren, I wanted to leave them a story of their grandfather, what he stood for, and the life lessons he learned along the way. I would have loved to have a book such as this from my grandfathers, as I know they both had intriguing lives to tell about. They are gone now, and their stories with them.

Once I started writing the book, and with some strong encouragement from friends, I decided to expand my audience from my family, relatives, and friends to others who might learn from the stories and spiritual applications.

Each chapter shares a real-life experience from my career, yet they are not in chronological order, and each stands on its own. Historical events are mentioned in the stories but are not the central theme. As my daughter stated, it is a book of short stories with spiritual application that can be set on your coffee table to read anytime.

We, Christians, are bad about compartmentalizing our lives into the spiritual and the physical. One world is work, friends, and family; the other is the church and possibly prayer and devotionals in the morning. But that is not the way God intends for us to live! As I have written this book, I have become very aware of how our spiritual and physical lives should fully intersect and integrate. We can learn spiritual lessons and applications in every day-to-day experience! When these two lives become one, we know we are walking in the Spirit as God intended.

As you read this book, I pray you will enjoy the stories but not miss what the Lord may say to you through the applications. I present this book not as someone who has it all together, but as somebody who is still on a spiritual journey and wants to use his platform to glorify God.

Introduction

TO THIS DAY, I remember where I was and what I was doing on November 22, 1963. I was five years old, living temporarily in Ft. Worth, Texas, and settling in to watch cartoons on our black and white television when the special report regarding the assassination of President John F. Kennedy came on. While I didn't understand the full implications of the event, I knew it was significant because my parents stayed glued to the television in silence all afternoon and evening.

Two days later, they loaded my two sisters and me into the car, and we drove the 25 miles to Dealey Plaza in Dallas, Texas, to see where this tragedy occurred. While I don't remember much about the trip, I do remember crowds of people milling around talking in hushed tones and the large grassy mound covered in flowers.

Over the next week, there seemed to be constant television coverage of events as they unfolded. But the next clear memory in my five-year-old mind was of the six white horses pulling the wagon with the candy-striped casket slowly down the road as crowds lined the street, many weeping. Who would have thought that years later I would be forever tied to this event and working for the organization whose primary responsibility was ensuring this tragedy never struck our nation again?

My story begins as a "missionary kid" raised in a Southern Baptist home. My earliest childhood memories are of Nassau, Bahamas, where my parents, Weldon and Joyce Viertel, were assigned as foreign missionaries. We often moved throughout my lifetime, but by the time I reached high school, we had settled in

El Paso, Texas, where my parents were assigned to the Baptist Spanish Publishing House. After graduation, I attended Howard Payne University in Brownwood, Texas, where I played basketball and majored in Secondary Education. It was here that I met my wife, Jan, and we were married in 1980.

I coached basketball for several years but felt restless and continued to be drawn to my childhood dream of being a federal law enforcement agent. I began to pursue that dream and, on a whim, walked into the small, obscure office of the Secret Service in Ft. Worth, Texas, to apply.

The story of how I was hired is a testimony to God's impeccable timing in our lives. After the Kennedy assassination, the Warren Commission Report determined that the Secret Service was undersized, operating at only 350 agents. In the aftermath of the tragedy, several hundred agents were hired, and the budget was drastically increased. Those agents hired in 1964 were coming up on retirement when I walked in to apply in 1983. The Secret Service was in the middle of a major hiring push when I showed up to apply with no law enforcement or military training or background.

While I don't want to bore you with all my different positions and assignments over the years, a brief summary of my career will shed some light on the following stories because they are not chronological but in random order. Without this background information, you may wonder why I am at the White House in one chapter and the next in the Dallas Field Office.

I spent the first six years of my career primarily working investigations in the Dallas, Texas, and then the Shreveport, Louisiana, offices of the Secret Service before being transferred to the Presidential Protective Division in Plains, Georgia. I served several years protecting former President and Mrs. Carter before moving to the protective division and working in the Clinton White House. After my protection assignments, I rose through the ranks, working in the Los Angeles and Memphis offices before being appointed a deputy assistant director back in Washington, D.C. Upon completing the assignment in Washington, D.C., I became the special agent in charge of the Chicago Field Office, retiring in 2008.

After I retired from the Secret Service, I worked for the Billy Graham Evangelistic Association and Samaritan's Purse. I eventually became vice president for Global Security for both organizations, retiring again in 2017.

My testimony is the same as many others raised in a Christian home. I accepted the Lord as a young boy and was baptized at the age of six. I was raised in the church and always active in youth groups which generally kept me out of trouble. My spiritual journey has gone through a few dry times during my life, but each time, the Lord has drawn me back to Himself, and my walk with Him grows closer daily.

One of my spiritual gifts is teaching, and as I've moved around the country with my career, we have belonged to some wonderful churches where I've had the privilege of teaching the Bible to high school and college students, as well as adult classes. The love of scripture has prompted me to write the following chapters, combining the amazing adventures God has allowed me to experience with his Word.

Redemption

---◆---

Therefore, if anyone is in Christ, the new creation has come: The old has gone, the new is here!
-2 Corinthians 5:17

THE SMALL TWIN-ENGINE plane made a low-altitude pass over the runway as the pilot scanned the landing strip for any new obstacles or bomb holes that might have appeared since the last time he landed here. Towards the end of the runway was an old burned-out Russian cargo plane, but there was enough runway available to land before reaching that obstruction. I could now see why the pilot weighed my luggage and then curiously insisted on me stepping on the scales before we boarded the small plane in the Ivory Coast. There wasn't much margin for error when landing on such a short runway.

The plane lightly touched down, and then the pilot immediately engaged the brakes to bring the aircraft to a stop as quickly as possible. We slowly taxied to a small metal structure adjacent to the abandoned airport where we were met by the U.S. State Department regional security officer. "Welcome to Monrovia!" he said as he handed my Secret Service partner and me flak jackets and helmets. "You don't need to wear them but always have them handy," he said. We loaded into the embassy vehicle and headed to the deserted U.S. Embassy.

It was October 1991, and I had traveled to the country of Liberia, West Africa, to make security and logistical arrangements for former President Jimmy Carter's visit to the war-torn country. A bloody war, which eventually claimed the lives of 150,000 Liberians, had broken out in 1989 when President Samuel Doe was captured, tortured by having his ears and fingers cut off, and then killed by a warlord named Prince Johnson. With the resulting power vacuum, numerous

1

entities were vying for domination, with Prince Johnson controlling most of the capital city of Monrovia and rebel leader Charles Taylor coming in from the south and holding most of the countryside. The third group was the West African Peace-keeping Force (ECOMOG), ill-equipped, undisciplined, and often part of the problem in the war-ravaged country. The purpose of President Carter's trip was to try to meet with each of the factions and move towards some type of resolution.

Getting there was somewhat of a problem since the American Embassy had been evacuated, and there were no commercial flights in or out of the country. The runways at the airport in Monrovia were full of bomb holes, but we eventually found a pilot with a small private airplane who could get us to Monrovia.

Over the next several days, arrangements were made for President Carter to meet with Prince Johnson and various peace-keeping officials at the embassy. The biggest challenge would be locating Charles Taylor somewhere out in the countryside. He traveled from village to village, and nobody knew where he was at any given time.

President Carter arrived midweek, and all scheduled meetings took place at the embassy. By the weekend, we still had not received any word from Charles Taylor regarding his location or whether he would be willing to meet. Finally, on Sunday afternoon, President Carter decided that he wanted to strike out into the countryside and see if we could find Taylor. While we were gravely concerned about heading out into unknown territory without any communications or military support, President Carter was determined to talk with Charles Taylor before leaving Liberia.

At about 2:00 in the afternoon, we departed the embassy in two embassy Suburbans, escorted by an ECOMOG jeep. It was a disconcerting feeling as we drove south out of Monrovia, through the ECOMOG checkpoints, and into the thick vegetation of the countryside. We were lightly armed compared to the weaponry we saw carried by the rebel fighters along our route.

Having an idea of the region Charles Taylor was in, we headed in that direction, stopping in every village and asking if Taylor and his fighters had been there. We got answers that he had been there between two and five days earlier, so we knew we were in the right area. We traveled from village to village that evening and into the night, searching for Taylor. Finally, at about 2:00 a.m. on Monday, we rolled into a village and were told that Charles Taylor was at a house just down the road. We pulled up to the place, which was bustling with activity, and escorted

President Carter to the front door. Two agents entered the house with the president while I took up position on the front porch. As my eyes fully adjusted to the dim light, I was astonished at what I saw. It was like a miniature army! A few adult fighters were sitting around, but most were kids who appeared between nine and thirteen years old, not much bigger than the rifles they carried.

With my 6'7" height, they were intrigued by how tall I was and cautiously took turns coming up and measuring themselves against me. Their ragged clothes gave me the impression that they were not well cared for, so I went to one of the vehicles and pulled out a case of MREs (meals ready to eat). I handed them out, and they tore into the food packets as if they hadn't had a good meal in a while. I sat down on the front porch, and they all stood back and stared at me, still trying to figure me out. At that moment, my eyes were opened to the depravity of man. These children should have been safely at home with their parents. Instead, many of them had watched as their parents and families were killed in terrible ways, after which they were conscripted into this army of fighters, given a gun, and taught to kill and maim. Their commanders had given them amulets and painted their young faces white, convincing them that this made them invisible to the enemy they were fighting. How could a loving God allow this to happen, and could He ever really forgive such wickedness?

One of the warlords who fought against Charles Taylor was Joshua Blahyi. He was legendary during the Liberian conflict and was known for fighting naked, wearing only shoes. He believed his nakedness protected him from his enemies, and the practice earned him the title "General Butt Naked." He was a Satanic priest who practiced child sacrifice and cannibalism to appease his Satanic idol. The things he did were too gruesome and wicked to record in this story, but the worst thing was that the fighters who followed him were primarily children and youth who participated in his Satanic rituals. His violence and hunger for killing earned him the title "most evil man in the world" as his legend grew.

One day in 1996, as the civil war raged on, Blahyi said that he was preparing to go into battle when a bright light appeared, and he had a vision of Jesus standing next to him. He recounted that Jesus spoke to him, saying, "Repent of your sins, or you will die." Shocked and petrified by the vision, Blahyi said that he turned to his young warriors and told them they would not fight that day.

For several weeks after this vision, he slept in the pews of a local church while being ministered to by the local pastor. And then, in early 1997, he escaped to a refugee camp in the neighboring country of Ghana. Here, he finally confessed his sins and became a true follower of Christ.

In February 2011, I had the chance to return to Monrovia, Liberia, for an evangelistic festival while working for Franklin Graham and the Billy Graham Evangelistic Association. We had been there several days when one of the videographers introduced me to a local pastor. We talked about his ministry and life during and after the civil war. His story sounded familiar. "General Butt Naked?" I asked. He looked down and replied, "No, he died long ago. I am a new man."

The question I had asked on that front porch in Liberia back in 1991 had been answered. Yes, our God can absolutely forgive such wickedness. He had forgiven "the most evil man in the world"! Today, Joshua Blahyi preaches the gospel and runs a home that houses and ministers to Liberia's former child soldiers while teaching them a trade.

Paul says, "Therefore, if anyone is in Christ, the new creation has come: The old has gone, the new is here!" (2 Corinthians 5:17). When a verse starts with the word therefore, we must go back to previous verses for context. Verse 15 tells us that "he died for all, that those who live should no longer live for themselves but for him who died for them and was raised again." Paul says that all true believers have died along with Christ, their old sinful natures being nailed to the cross. That nature was then buried with Christ, and a new nature was resurrected with Christ. This new creation no longer serves itself but serves Him who died for us. Paul says it another way: "We were therefore buried with him through baptism into death in order that, just as Christ was raised from the dead through the glory of the Father, we too may live a new life" (Romans 6:4).

To really appreciate this truth, we must realize that this new life we enjoy is a new creation of God, not a remodel of the old life; that one no longer exists. The new life was created through the will and work of God, not through our own efforts or heritage. John says we are "children born not of natural descent, nor of human decision or a husband's will, but born of God" (John 1:13). This is how Joshua Blahyi could consider himself a new person. While he had many regrets, he could honestly say that the evil man of the past is dead, buried, and gone!

Many in Liberia and the media do not believe Blahyi's conversion experience. They say that there is no way a person can make that type of transformation. But that is the miracle of regeneration Paul talks about in 2 Corinthians. I'm sure many who knew Paul before his conversion forever had doubts about the sincerity of his ministry. But our God is in the business of redeeming those who are lost. It was no more of a miracle for him to deliver Paul or Joshua Blahyi than it was for him to redeem you or me. The same amount of blood was needed for Joshua Blahyi's salvation as was needed for mine.

Father, thank You for the new identity You have given us in Christ. Please help us let go of the old nature and things of the past and press on to the new things You have set before us. Thank You that our new identity allows us to wake up every day with a fresh start because of the forgiveness offered us through Your son and His death on the cross. Amen.

Thanks for the Tour

—————— ✦ ——————

Therefore, as God's chosen people, holy and dearly loved, clothe yourselves with compassion, kindness, humility, gentleness and patience.
–Colossians 3:12

TO ALL OF us in the Secret Service who had the privilege of being around her, former First Lady Barbara Bush was a favorite. Even though I was never permanently on her security detail, I was in her presence enough to experience her genuineness.

One such occasion was in 1986 when I was a very young agent in the Ft. Worth, Texas, office. At that time, Mrs. Bush was the Second Lady of the United States, and her husband was the vice president under President Reagan. She was scheduled to fly into Ft. Worth late one night, stay at a private residence, and attend a function the next morning. I was assigned to be the lead advance for her two-day visit to Ft. Worth, which meant I was responsible for motorcades, site security, and coordination with the airport and local police jurisdictions. Since I would be driving her limo, I ran all of the primary motorcade, alternate, and hospital routes numerous times during the days leading up to her visit. This was my first protective advance, and I did not want to mess it up!

On the day of her visit, Mrs. Bush arrived at the airport by private plane at about 9:00 p.m. I met her with the limo at the bottom of the aircraft steps, and she and her young assistant climbed into the limo's back seat while her detail leader took the front seat. She was very cordial, asking my name, where I was from, and how many children I had.

As we left the airport, she and her assistant settled into the back seat and began discussing her schedule, future travel, and other personal things. As we got closer to the city and the residence where she would be staying, I began to get an uneasy feeling. Things did not look as familiar as when I repeatedly drove the motorcade routes before her arrival. I discovered I had broken the cardinal rule of a good motorcade agent; always rehearse the route at the same time of day that you will actually be driving the protectee. Things look very different at night than they do by day. I made several turns in the direction I thought we were supposed to go, but nothing looked familiar. I felt the hair on the back of my neck stand up; I was lost! Not having Google Maps or GPS in those days, I glanced down at the city street map sitting on the seat next to my right leg, seeing if I could find a way back out to the main street. I looked in the rearview mirror, and Mrs. Bush and her assistant were still deep in conversation. All I could think was, "I can't stop and turn around because then they will know that I am lost!"

I made several more turns and eventually saw a major road ahead of us. As we got closer to the intersection, I began to get my bearings. We made a right at the traffic light, and thankfully, we were back on the correct route. I again glanced in the mirror and saw that Mrs. Bush was still absorbed in conversation. As we pulled up to the residence, I felt pretty proud of myself. But then, as Mrs. Bush was getting out of the car, she leaned forward, patted me on the shoulder with a sly smile on her face, and said, "Thanks for the tour!"

This was the type of response that elicited so much love and admiration for Mrs. Bush. It was late at night, she had to be up early the following day, and she was being greatly inconvenienced. Yet she saw a young agent struggling and chose kindness, compassion, and patience. This was not the typical response from those in positions of power and status.

As I watched the media coverage of her funeral in 2018, I heard story after story of the compassion and kindness Mrs. Bush had shown during her lifetime, and my mind went back to that night in Ft. Worth when she extended grace to me.

Our world is a mess. The constant bombardment of political conflict, gun violence, racial unrest, and videos of anarchy in the streets have hardened our hearts toward others. We take sides on every issue and condemn anyone who believes differently. Kindness seems to be obsolete as everybody is out to take care of themselves. Yet Paul says that as a result of God's extreme love for us, we should "clothe (y)ourselves with compassion, kindness, humility, gentleness, and patience" (Colossians 3:12). This is a significant part of the sanctification process and becoming more like Christ. If we are not striving daily to be kind and compassionate, we need to question our true commitment to Christ.

But Paul goes on to say, "And over all these virtues put on love, which binds them all together in perfect unity" (Colossians 3:14). He draws a picture of "clothing" ourselves in compassion, kindness, humility, gentleness, and patience, and then putting on a "coat" of love over these virtues. This cloak or "girdle" keeps all these other virtues in place. Without this outer garment of love holding everything together, we will never be consistent in trying to demonstrate the other Christlike qualities we are to have. Paul further emphasizes this point when he says, "If I give all I possess to the poor and surrender my body to the flames, but have not love, I gain nothing" (1 Corinthians 13:3).

Kindness is not an easy task because so many people are unlovable. It will require the supernatural power of the Holy Spirit within us to take on the characteristics and the extreme love Paul describes in this passage. To do this, every day we need to recommit ourselves and ask the Holy Spirit to empower us to take on the attributes of Christ. Without His help, we are destined to fail.

Father, we get so caught up in today's divisive rhetoric that we have forgotten the basic qualities of being a Christ-follower: compassion, kindness, humility, gentleness, and patience. How can we expect the world to want what we have when we cannot even get the basics right? Holy Spirit, convict us of the way we treat people as we come in contact with them daily. Please help us to realize that as Christians, the world is watching, and our actions often speak louder than words. Amen.

True Worship

————————— ✦ —————————

Yet a time is coming and has now come when the true worshipers will worship the Father in the Spirit and in truth, for they are the kind of worshipers the Father seeks.
-John 4:23

HOW OFTEN DO we Christians rate a worship experience by the quality or style of music or the emotional responses to a sermon? We believe that if we enjoyed it, surely God accepted it as worthy praise. We go to some worship services, don't like the music, the preacher is dull with no good stories or memorable catchphrases, and we feel like we have wasted our time. But when did worship become about us?

I surmise that the main reason we experience these "worship failures" is that we did not show up with an attitude of praise and worship. If we have gone through the entire week without any real communion with God, and we enter the auditorium visiting, talking, laughing, and high-fiving, we can't expect to suddenly turn it on when the first song starts on a Sunday morning. True worship takes the preparation of our hearts, whether it be a confession of sins or reflection on the greatness of God and who He is as the Creator of the universe.

I was convicted of this during a visit to Nyankunde, a small village of approximately 11,000 in the Democratic Republic of Congo. There is a hospital there called Evangelical Medical Center, supported by Samaritan's Purse. It is the only hospital in that region of the country, and it serves people who come from miles away to seek medical attention. Today, it is a peaceful little village, but that was not always the case.

In 2002, during the height of the civil war in Congo, the people of Nyankunde were attacked by a neighboring tribe intent on annihilating the village. Seven thousand militiamen armed with guns, machetes, and spears descended from the surrounding hillside, killing everyone in their path, including women and children. They entered the 200-bed hospital and killed anyone they could find in the hallways and hospital beds. Bodies lay everywhere in the streets, and those who were not killed were taken to a large warehouse and locked inside, where they were left to dehydrate and starve to death. The siege lasted for several days while the attackers looted anything of value and destroyed the hospital and houses in the community. Some were able to escape, but up to 4,500 people were massacred in the village. It became a ghost town as militias continued to come through and loot for several months after the attack and then placed landmines throughout the village.

Eventually, in 2005, United Nations Peacekeepers came through and demined the village, and people slowly came back. They found the hospital destroyed and very little left of their community. The recovery process was slow, but Samaritan's Purse stepped in and provided funding to repair the hospital, including a new operating room and intensive care facilities. Soon the hospital was in business again.

In 2012, as part of my security duties with Samaritan's Purse, I visited the hospital in Nyankunde to make sure we had an emergency, contingency, and evacuation plan in place for our personnel if there was another attack or similar disaster. We were there over a Sunday and were invited by the hospital staff to attend church services with them, which we were more than happy to do.

As we approached the church, I noticed that it was simply a metal roof held up by wooden posts. There were no walls, and it was furnished with old, rough wooden pews. I watched as people dressed in their best clothes converged on the church from all directions. As they entered the church, they talked in low whispers, if they spoke at all. As they took their place in the pews, they bowed their heads either in meditation or prayer. There was no piano, platform, sound system, or pulpit. A rickety lectern was all that stood at the front of the church. We sat in complete silence for about ten minutes while people filed in and took their places. Then a man in the front row began to sing and the congregation behind him joined in the most beautiful four-part harmony I had ever heard. I glanced at the faces of the people as they lifted their heartfelt praise and noticed their eyes were closed or they were looking upward. I was amazed to see there were no spectators; everyone was engaged. As a song would end, the man on the front pew would pause for a few moments before starting another. No instruments, no drums, no praise team, no special lighting effects; just us and God.

I don't know how many songs we sang, but the praise and worship crescendoed and seemed to climax with the final verse of Rock of Ages:

> While I draw this fleeting breath,
> When mine eyes shall close in death,
> When I soar to worlds unknown,
> See Thee on Thy judgement throne,
> Rock of Ages, cleft for me,
> Let me hide myself in Thee.

As I looked around, there was not a dry eye in the place. Most of these people had lost loved ones in the terrible massacre—children, parents, brothers, sisters, aunts, uncles, and close friends. Yet they sang with assurance and confidence that their Rock of Ages was a strong tower in which they could take refuge, no matter their situation.

The pastor stood and preached from the book of John, and then we sang another hymn before dismissing. It was early afternoon before we were through, but I found myself wanting to linger in what I had just experienced. There was no urge to rush out of the church to get in line at a restaurant. These people had captured the power of true worship, and it was not something they showed up to do; it was something they lived and brought with them.

Jesus said that the Father is seeking "true worshippers" who will worship "in spirit and in truth." I have often read this scripture without catching its true meaning. We have churches that worship in "spirit" with little attention given to the truth. They have a heartfelt passion for God, but the depth of their knowledge of God is shallow. On the other hand, we have churches that worship in "truth" with little attention given to worshipping in the Spirit. These churches tend to be rich in theology and knowledge but dry, legalistic, and without passion. A middle ground between both of these extremes is what Jesus was talking about when He said we are to worship in spirit and in truth, and there is only one way to accomplish this. Sunday morning worship must be a continuation of our lifestyle of praise and worship. We shouldn't go to church on Sunday to worship; we should bring our worship with us.

———————————

Lord, You are indeed worthy of our worship not just on Sunday, but every waking moment of every day. Our lives should be lived in an attitude of praise and thanksgiving where Sunday is just a continuation of the praise we offer you all week. As the song says, take us back to the heart of worship, for it's all about You. Forgive us for making it about us. Amen.

———————————

He Knows My Name!

———— ✦ ————

"The gatekeeper opens the gate for him, and the sheep listen to his voice. He calls his own sheep by name and leads them out."
-John 10:3

I COME FROM a long line of ranchers in Texas. One of those ranchers was my Uncle A.J., who raised cattle in George West, Texas. When he and my Aunt Patsy would go out to check on the newborn calves, he had a strict rule: Do not name the calves! Why? Once you start calling a calf by a name, it becomes a personal relationship rather than a business asset.

In late 1993, I was transferred to the White House detail, where I became a member of a group of men and women assigned the responsibility of protecting President Clinton and his family. There was a lot to learn, and I often felt overwhelmed by the responsibility. I watched as many of the agents who had been there for a while moved around with confidence and ease, and they had a comradery from years of working with each other. I was a little intimidated and felt like an outsider, wondering how long it would take for me to fit in.

Since I was a pretty good runner, I was assigned as one of the agents who would accompany President Clinton on his morning runs through Washington, D.C. I was a little nervous about this part of my assignment, worrying that I would do something wrong or not do something I was supposed to. It did not help that the White House press pool was constantly videoing the president on his runs, and any little slip-up on my part could end up on national news.

One morning, a couple of weeks into this assignment, I was standing on the first floor of the White House residence, waiting for the president to come down for his run. Suddenly, the elevator doors opened, and out stepped President Clinton in his running attire. He looked me squarely in the eyes and with a smile, said, "Good morning, Tim." My chest swelled with pride, and all I could think was that he knew my name! It wasn't just "good morning" or "good morning, agent." It was "good morning, Tim." Suddenly, everything was right. I was part of the team. The leader of the free world personally knew my name.

There is a scientific reason why I felt that rush. It is a proven fact that when we hear our name called by someone, feel-good hormones like dopamine and serotonin are released into our brains, resulting in feelings of excitement and self-worth. The more esteemed and respected the person who calls our name is, the bigger the rush of excitement. It's the difference between hearing your name from a friend and hearing it from a high-ranking leader in your company, or in my case, the president. Our names are personal and separate us from the crowd. Without names, we are just a face or a number, which doesn't encourage our self-worth.

Jesus said, "Very truly I tell you Pharisees, anyone who does not enter the sheep pen by the gate, but climbs in by some other way, is a thief and a robber. The one who enters by the gate is the shepherd of the sheep. The gatekeeper opens the gate for him, and the sheep listen to his voice. He calls his own sheep by name and leads them out. When he has brought out all his own, he goes on ahead of them, and his sheep follow him because they know his voice" (John 10:1–4). The analogy that Jesus uses in this passage is of Himself, the caring shepherd, coming to the sheep pen gate. In those days, a gatekeeper would lay across the entrance to keep anyone or anything that would harm the sheep from entering the pen. Usually, there were several different flocks in the pen that could be watched by one gatekeeper. Jesus says that the shepherd calls his own sheep by name, and he leads them out. Not all of the sheep followed him out, just those that he knew by name and who personally recognized the shepherd.

Three things I take away from this passage. First, unlike the relationship between a rancher and his calves, Jesus wants to know our names. I cannot even fathom the image of Jesus standing at the sheep pen gate, pointing with His staff, and saying, "You, you, and you, come with me." No, He wants a personal relationship with us, and the only way He can have that is by knowing and calling our names. My uncle did not want that personal relationship with his calves because he knew it would not be an enduring one. The calf would have to be sold or sent to the butcher at some point, and the relationship would be cut short. On the other hand, Jesus the Good Shepherd is in this relationship for the long haul—eternity!

Second, how often do we take for granted that we know the Creator of the universe? Think about that! Many people will claim to know famous stars, athletes, or politicians when they actually shook their hands and had only a short conversation once. That person has probably never thought of them since! On the other hand, Jesus said "his sheep follow him because they know his voice." This describes an intimate relationship, not a one-time handshake! The Psalmist said, "You have searched me, Lord, and you know me. You know when I sit and when I rise; you perceive my thoughts from afar. You discern my going out and my lying down; you are familiar with all my ways. Before a word is on my tongue you, Lord, know it completely. You hem me in behind and before, and you lay your hand upon me. Such knowledge is too wonderful for me, too lofty for me to attain" (Psalm 139:1–6).

Third, He identified and chose us, not vice versa. I have had friends who have pursued relationships with important people until they finally noticed them. The relationship ends up one-sided, with my friend constantly vying for attention. This is not the nature of our relationship with Jesus. He said, "He calls his own sheep by name and leads them out." He chose us! We do not have to chase after Him to get His attention.

I got all giddy about the president knowing my name, but it was never an intimate or lasting relationship that he valued. On the other hand, the Creator of the universe chose me, knows my name, and values me. Just the thought of that should give me a rush of excitement and self-worth!

―――――――――――――

Jesus, thank you that you want an intimate relationship with each one of us. As the good shepherd, You care for us daily by ensuring that we have what we need. You bind up our wounds when we are hurt or injured, and we are never out of Your sight. Thank You for the assurance that comes from the knowledge that You know us each by name. Amen.

―――――――――――――

Going to the Big House

---◆---

For the wages of sin is death, but the gift of God is eternal life.
-Romans 6:23

FOOD STAMP FRAUD in the United States has always been an issue, but in the late 1990s, federal law enforcement decided to take a different approach to fight it. Until then, the focus had been on arresting the food stamp recipients who were selling their monthly allotment of food stamps for cash instead of using the stamps to feed their families. The new tactic was to go after the dirty retailers who were purchasing the food stamps from the recipients for fifty to eighty cents on the dollar. They would then deposit the food stamps in their business bank accounts and receive the full face value of the food stamps from the U.S. government. It had turned into a lucrative scam for dishonest retailers. We would identify and target stores based on the number of food stamps they ran through the system every month versus regular cash deposits and compare these amounts with actual inventory on their shelves. Some of these stores were depositing more food stamps every month than they had products on the shelves.

We found one such store in a tiny rural town in Louisiana with a population of less than three hundred. It was located in an impoverished parish where many residents were receiving food stamp supplements. Records showed that a large portion of the food stamps issued in that parish was going through that store's bank account every month, amounting to thousands and thousands of dollars.

I put on an old T-shirt and some jeans, drove to the store in an old pickup, and went inside to look around. It didn't take long to see that there was probably less than $5,000 worth of inventory in the store, and many of the cans and food packages were dusty as if they had been there a while. An older man was behind the cash register with his elderly wife, sitting at a small table next to the counter. I tried to engage them in conversation, but both seemed reluctant to talk much with a stranger. I purchased my Coke and walked out. I could tell it was going to be very difficult to get them to deal with someone they did not recognize or know.

The next day, I stopped in at the local sheriff's office to tell them what we were up to and advise them that we were investigating the owners of the small store. The sheriff agreed that it would be very difficult to get the couple to deal with any outsiders but offered up a local informant he had used from time to time. We thought it was worth a try, so we gave the informant a book of stamps and sent him into the store. Ten minutes later, he came out with $50 cash he had received for the $100 book of stamps. A few days later, we gave the informant a few more books of stamps, but this time the serial numbers were recorded, and the stamps were surreptitiously marked. Again, the informant came out of the store with the cash he was paid for the stamps.

Several days later, we got a call from the Federal Reserve Bank telling us that they had recovered the marked stamps and that they had come through the target store's bank account. A couple weeks went by, and we decided to send the informant back into the store to sell more stamps. This time he went in with an undercover agent he introduced as his "friend" and identified her as the source of the food stamps he had been selling at the store. This time, we took a video/audio recording of the transaction, and we watched as the store owner took the stamps from the undercover agent, counted them out, and gave her cash. The undercover agent told the store owner that she had a source for a lot more stamps but needed to get at least 70 cents on the dollar because her source was demanding more money. The store owner hesitated but finally agreed to the new price. Later that week, the Federal Reserve Bank again contacted us and said that the stamps sold to the store by the undercover agent had been deposited in the target store's bank account.

Over the next several weeks, we did more deals with both store owners, all recorded on video. By this time, we had plenty of evidence, so we decided that we would do one more big deal and make the arrest. The undercover agent entered the store with a grocery bag full of stamps, and even on the video, we could see both the store owner's and his wife's eyes light up. As he greedily emptied the grocery sack full of stamps onto the counter and started counting them out, he chuckled and said, "If I get caught doing this, I'm going to the Big House!"

We arrested the man and his wife, and within a couple of weeks, they were indicted for food stamp fraud and money laundering. The defense attorney appealed to the court's mercy, saying that his clients were elderly, didn't know that what they were doing was illegal, and were entrapped. In response, the U.S. attorney played the video of the final undercover transaction: "If I get caught doing this, I'm going to the Big House." The man's flippant attitude about the crime and its consequences returned to haunt him, and he and his wife had no choice but to plead guilty to the charges.

On the day of sentencing, I watched as the elderly couple stood holding hands in front of the federal judge sitting behind the massive bench. They looked diminutive standing there, and as I watched them, I felt pity for them. The scene reminded me of what it must have looked like when Adam and Eve stood before God, awaiting his judgment on their seemingly insignificant sin of eating a piece of fruit. I found myself hoping the judge would be lenient with them, but that would not be the case. The judge gave each of them five years of federal time for their crimes. Upon hearing the sentence, the wife started sobbing loudly as her husband tried to comfort her. Clearly, neither one expected to get any prison time for what they thought was a menial crime. As the judge handed down the sentence, he referred to the flippant statement the man had made about breaking the law. Undoubtedly, the judge felt the man was making light of the seriousness of his crime and the punishment he might receive if he were caught.

In the same way, the world has a way of mocking God's judgment. They say that a truly loving God would never send anyone to Hell. The enemy has deceived them into thinking that God will overlook sin as long as it hasn't been too serious. But Paul warns, "Do not be deceived, God is not mocked [He will not allow Himself to be ridiculed, nor treated with contempt nor allow His precepts to be scornfully set aside]; for whatever a man sows, this and this only is what he will reap" (Galatians 6:7 AMP). His judgment will be sure and swift, and He does not judge on a sliding scale. Sins are sins. In God's judicial system, lying (even the little white lies) is just as wrong as sexual immorality, stealing, or murder. There are no minor or menial sins. Our lives will be laid bare before Him on the Day of Judgement. Not only will we be accountable for public sins we have committed, but also the private ones, including impure motives, thoughts, and actions we always thought we had gotten away with. When we fully and truly understand this, we will marvel at the wonder and glory of the cross!

Let's imagine if someone of great influence had walked into the courtroom at the time of the elderly couple's sentencing, approached the bench, and whispered something in the judge's ear. The judge slams his gavel and declares, "Your sentences have been commuted; you are free to go." The joy, elation, and relief of that couple would have been indescribable! One moment, they were facing the possibility of spending the rest of their lives in prison; now, they were walking out free. This is the magnificence of the cross and what Jesus has done for those of us who follow Him. Without Him, our sentences have already been determined. God will not be mocked!

Lord, forgive us for imposing our standards on You for what is fair or unfair. You are a just God who hates sin and will judge every wrong. At the same time, You are a loving God who has provided a way of salvation for every one of us to escape the wrath of your judgment. Lord, may we fully grasp the gravity of our sins and the miracle of the cross that has rescued us from eternal separation from You. Amen.

An Unsung Hero

—————◆—————

Do nothing out of selfish ambition or vain conceit. Rather, in humility value others above yourselves, not looking to your own interests but each of you to the interests of the others.
-Philippians 2:3–4

FOR JERRY PARR, the special agent in charge of the presidential protective division during the Reagan Administration, what started out as a typical day ended in a national drama. It was March 30, 1981, and Jerry was performing his usual duty of accompanying President Reagan whenever he left the White House. On this date, they went to the Washington Hilton in Washington, D.C., for a speech to the AFL-CIO Labor Union. If there ever was a routine visit of the president to a location, this was it. For years the hotel had been used for major political functions, and the Secret Service knew the hotel inside and out because of the numerous times presidents had visited there. A private side entrance was always used because the motorcade could pull up to a point where there were only thirty feet between the door and the president's limo.

On this particular day, the Secret Service had allowed the general public to line up on the sidewalk outside the private entrance, a little closer than they should have. As President Reagan emerged with Jerry Parr working his left shoulder, six shots rang out, all fired by John Hinckley within 1.7 seconds. By the time the second shot was fired, Jerry had already grabbed the president and shoved him toward the limo's open door. Jerry piled in on top of the president, the door was slammed shut, and the limo raced off.

Initially, Jerry thought the president was uninjured and ordered the driver to head back to the White House, where the president's personal physician could thoroughly check the president to make sure he was indeed okay. The president complained of his ribs hurting but thought he injured them as he was being pushed into the vehicle. But then Jerry saw a small amount of frothy blood in the corner of President Reagan's mouth and knew immediately the sign of a punctured lung. He directed the driver to get them to George Washington Hospital as quickly as possible. When they arrived at the emergency entrance to the hospital, President Reagan tried to walk into the hospital on his own but collapsed just inside the emergency room door.

Once they got President Reagan on the examination table, they found he was hemorrhaging internally from a bullet wound. Apparently, the sixth round fired from Hinckley's gun hit the right rear quarter panel of the limo, flattening it out to the size of a dime. The round then traveled through the small crack between the body of the limo and the open door and struck President Reagan in the side as he was being pushed into the vehicle. The dime-shaped round entered between two ribs, punctured a lung, and came to rest about an inch from his heart. According to the doctors at George Washington Hospital, had Jerry Parr not made the quick decision to divert to the hospital, President Reagan would have died back at the White House from the loss of blood. Jerry Parr was an unsung hero whose quick thinking probably changed the course of history. Yet Jerry was the humblest man you would ever meet.

I first met Jerry Parr in 1984. He was the keynote speaker at the graduation ceremony for my class of twenty-three newly trained special agents. Jerry was a legend in the Secret Service, and I expected a flamboyant, brash, impeccably dressed man delivering a "win one for the Gipper" kind of speech. Jerry was none of that. He came across as a reserved, thoughtful man with loads of wisdom. We hung on to every word, and to this day, I remember his words regarding our call to duty and service to the people of this country. After the ceremony, he stayed around for a while to visit and take photos with each graduate. I still have that prized photo to this day!

Matthew 5:5 says, "Blessed are the meek, for they will inherit the earth." In today's world, meekness is considered weakness, timidity, or faintheartedness. But that is not what Jesus was referring to when he used it in the Sermon on the Mount. The word translated as "meek" was used by the Greeks to describe a powerful horse that had been broken. It was power and strength under control. A meek person exudes quiet confidence and calm humility. They know who they are and where they are going. They don't need the approval or adoration of man. Our model for meekness and humility was Jesus, and I perceived this attribute in Jerry Parr.

Jerry Parr retired from the Secret Service in 1985. With his resume, past experiences, and notoriety, he could have had his choice of big-time positions with any number of private companies. But he chose a road few would choose. He became a pastor in an inner-city church in Washington, D.C. He chose to serve the hungry, the homeless, and the orphans and share the love of Jesus Christ. He once drove a school bus full of supplies 3,000 miles to an orphanage in San Salvador. While many of his peers were enjoying lucrative jobs in the private sector, Jerry Parr was humbly laying up treasures in heaven.

The last time I saw Jerry was a Sunday morning in 1994 as we were bringing President and Mrs. Clinton back to the White House from church services at Foundry Methodist. Our route took us through a small side street adjacent to Lafayette Park across from the White House. As the elaborate motorcade rolled by the park with all of its pomp and circumstance, I saw Jerry standing behind a folding table, handing out meals to the homeless. The mind will sometimes take a snapshot of something, and that image becomes stamped into memory. My mind did just that. The image of Jerry Parr in Lafayette Park on that day is embedded in my memory under the caption "humility."

Lord, humility, and meekness are not traits that the world values today, but Your Word says that they are what we, as followers of Christ, should strive to be. Help us see that these qualities are not signs of weakness or cowardice but power under control. Show us that true meekness is incompatible with pride, ego, and self-centeredness, which we all struggle with. Thank You for Your example of meekness and humility as You gave up all to come to earth to rescue us from our sins. Amen.

The Face of God

---◆---

When I consider your heavens, the work of your fingers, the moon
and the stars, which you have set in place, what is mankind that
you are mindful of them, human beings that you care for them?
-Psalm 8:3–4

THE EVENTS OF January 28, 1986, are indelibly marked in the memory of all of us who are old enough to remember. Most of us recall where we were and what we were doing when we got the news that the Space Shuttle Challenger had exploded soon after takeoff from Cape Canaveral. I rushed to the Dallas Secret Service Field Office, where I was assigned, and watched the video clips in disbelief as the powerful rocket booster launched and powered the space shuttle into space in a picture-perfect takeoff. But 73 seconds into the liftoff, as the shuttle was just about out of sight, there was a puff of smoke, and then three or four large vapor trails as the aircraft broke into pieces and started hurtling back to earth. The biggest heartbreak was watching the faces of family and close friends as they went from elation and excitement to the sudden shock of what was taking place. Also impacted were many children across the nation as televisions had been wheeled into classrooms for them to watch the launch. Schools had a special interest in this particular mission because Christa McAuliffe, a schoolteacher, was a crew member and was scheduled to conduct experiments and teach several lessons from space.

As the event unfolded, President Reagan was at the White House preparing to address the nation in his annual State of the Union later that evening. That speech was quickly canceled, and the president turned his attention to addressing and reassuring the country in one of his most famous speeches. He honored the seven crew members as heroes and comforted the children who had witnessed the tragedy on television. He ended his speech by saying, "We will never forget them, nor the last time we saw them, this morning, as they prepared for their journey and waved goodbye and 'slipped the surly bonds of earth' to 'touch the face of God.'"

The following day, I received a message that I was on a list of agents who needed to report to Houston, Texas, as soon as possible. President Reagan was scheduled to speak at a memorial service for the seven astronauts at the Johnson Space Center on January 31. I hurried home, packed my bags, and headed south to Houston.

On the morning of the memorial service, I received my posting assignment in the "Holding Room," where President and Mrs. Reagan would meet privately with the spouses and young children of the seven astronauts. I got there early as the sweeps were being completed and took up my position inside the room as the family members arrived. Needless to say, the mood in the room was somber, talk done in whispers. I could tell that reality had not set in for some of the younger children, while some of the older children seemed to be trying to comprehend what was happening.

As President and Mrs. Reagan arrived in the room, they spent time with each family member and child, talking, listening, and embracing. The tenderness and empathy he shared with each one were so genuine, and the surreal sight of the most powerful man in the world gently comforting the children was an experience I will never forget. This was a type of comfort they could receive from nowhere else. Many had offered words of comfort, but the fact that the president of the United States would take the time to learn their names, give them a physical touch, and let them know he sincerely cared was reassuring.

In the same way, as I was struck by the image of the powerful bending to comfort the small and insignificant, David was in awe that the God of the universe would bend to comfort and care for us. He said, "When I consider your heavens, the work of your fingers, the moon and the stars, which you have set in place, what is mankind that you are mindful of them, human beings that you care for them?" (Psalm 8:3–4).

As a ten-year-old boy, I remember Christmas Eve in 1968, watching with amazement as Apollo 8 circled the moon for the first time. As they came from the moon's backside, we all witnessed the first "earthrise" seen by man. While the world watched in wonder, the crew of Frank Borman, Jim Lovell, and Bill Anders started reading the creation account from Genesis 1: "In the beginning, God created the heavens and the earth . . ."

This was my Psalm 8 moment! How could a God responsible for creating something like this have a personal interest in a young boy who was just an insignificant mere speck on that giant blue globe? This is the wonder David felt even though he didn't have the scope of information we have today regarding the majesty of God's creation. He did not know that the earth was traveling at 67,000 miles per hour around the sun or rotating at 1,000 miles per hour. He saw several hundred stars in the sky while we now know there are several hundred billion in our galaxy. He never realized that the earth maintains a path around the sun at a perfect distance to keep us from burning up or freezing. Still, he marveled that a powerful Creator would care so much for insignificant human beings.

Unfortunately, with the advance in technology and science, we have lost a lot of the wonder of God's creation and the majesty of His name. With so many distractions, we rarely just sit and contemplate God's greatness while observing a sunset or gazing at a star-filled sky. We've lost that child-like sense of excitement over seeing a mountain for the first time or observing the intricate detail of a simple flower. Regrettably, when we take for granted the creation, we no longer marvel at the Creator and His love for us. Paul said it best: "For since the creation of the world God's invisible qualities—his eternal power and divine nature—have been clearly seen, being understood from what has been made, so that people are without excuse" (Romans 1:20). While the majesty of God is on full display daily through His creation, His love and concern for each of us was displayed on the cross.

Any of us would appreciate the most powerful man in the world canceling his schedule to comfort and care for us as President Reagan did for the grieving children. How much more should we, like David, marvel that the Creator of the universe is never too busy for His children and that we are always on His mind.

Father, we say with David how majestic is Your name in all of the earth! May we always wonder and marvel at Your power and creation and never forget Your tender mercies. Thank you for the love and care You show us as Your children and joint heirs with Your son. Amen.

Not Camel Again!

---◆---

The rabble with them began to crave other food, and again the
Israelites started wailing and said, "If only we had meat to eat! We
remember the fish we ate in Egypt at no cost—also the cucumbers,
melons, leeks, onions, and garlic. But now we have lost our appetite;
we never see anything but this manna!"
-Numbers 11:4–6

IN NUMBERS 11, the Israelites were once again complaining to Moses, this time about the free lunch program they were on. Verse 4 indicates that the grumbling was started by the "rabble" on the outskirts of the camp. Who was this rabble? These were probably non-Jews who accompanied the Israelites when they left Egypt. It is unknown why they left Egypt with God's chosen people, but it could have been one of three reasons. They could have been enamored of this mighty God of the Israelites, they could have wanted to leave before they got caught up in any more plagues, or they were just malcontents who weren't happy in Egypt. The latter seems to be the most likely reason since they were the first to express discontentment over the food situation. However, the Israelites were more than happy to join in and turn the grumbling into "wailing." I find it humorous that they said they received the food in Egypt at "no cost," as if they had to pay God for the manna they received every morning. But before we are too hard on the Israelites, we must do some honest self-examination.

In 2011, the Horn of Africa was in the worst drought seen in sixty years. Somalia was especially hard hit, and refugees poured across the Kenyan border in an attempt to make the sixty-seven-mile trek to Dadaab, Kenya, where there were two United Nations Refugee Camps that had been established in 1991. The capacity for these two camps was 90,000, but with the food and water shortage in 2011, the camps had swelled to over 400,000. Once the refugees made it to the camps, they found food and water, but thousands were dying on their way, a significant portion of these women and children. Samaritan's Purse responded to the area to help the traveling refugees between the Somalian border and the U.N. camps in Dadaab. The terrorist group Al-Shabaab was very active in that area, so Samaritan's Purse asked if I would go over and establish security measures and protocols for their operation in Dadaab. Having retired from the Secret Service for a while and looking for a way to serve, I readily agreed to go.

I flew to a small airstrip in Garissa, Kenya, where I was met by the Samaritan's Purse response manager for the three-hour drive of 67 miles to Dadaab. The road was not paved and, for the most part, was just two tracks through deep sand. I settled into the back seat and started taking in my surroundings. Because of the drought, there was no grass left, and along the way, I saw the carcasses of hundreds of sheep, goats, and other livestock. There were some brushy trees along the road, and to my utter amazement, goats were in the top of these trees 10 or 15 feet off the ground, grazing on the few leaves they could find.

As we pulled into our base in Dadaab, I could see I had much work to do in getting our security up to the level it needed to be. Most of the other relief organizations in Dadaab had served in the two United Nations refugee camps for a while. Their facilities had ten-foot walls, with security personnel posted at the entrance gates. Samaritan's Purse was operating out of a one-story residence with nothing but a hedge surrounding the property.

That evening, we had a meal that consisted of lean meat cut into one-inch cubes, rice, and beans. The meat was not bad, even though it was pretty tough and didn't have much taste. I usually didn't ask what it was because I really did not want to know. I established that practice after a trip to northern Congo, where I was given a choice between hippopotamus and bushmeat (a large rodent). However, soon after I finished my plate, the local lady hired to cook for us came over and asked how I enjoyed the camel. I complimented her cooking, feeling rather relieved. In my mind, the camel was somewhat more palatable than hippo or rat!

Early the following day, I went to the local police chief to introduce myself and inquire about the possibility of hiring some of his off-duty officers for armed security. He was accommodating and offered up ten of his reserve officers, all former military, to provide 24-hour protection for our base.

That afternoon, I went out looking for a local contractor who could build an eight-foot wall around our half-acre compound. The owner of the property we were leasing recommended a man, and I was able to track him down in Dadaab. He came out, looked at the property, and after agreeing to a price, said that he would be able to start work on the wall the following day.

The next day, it appeared that things were coming together. We had our armed security in place, which allowed us to rest easier, especially at night, and the contractor had shown up and was well on his way to getting our wall built. Then our worst fears were realized. I got a frantic call from one of our young employees returning to the base from his work in the field when he and his driver were ambushed. As they were coming through a narrow area in the road several miles outside of Dadaab, someone opened fire on them, striking their four-wheel-drive vehicle numerous times. Instead of stopping, the well-trained driver accelerated out of the "kill zone," and they were able to get away from the hail of bullets. I asked him if he and the driver were okay. He said that besides some cuts from flying glass, he thought they were both uninjured. I told him to go straight to the police station, and I would meet them there.

An inspection of the vehicle at the police station determined that seven rounds had hit the car. One of the rounds had hit the windshield while another one had gone through the passenger side window, missing our employee by a matter of inches. The police said there was not much they could do since the attack took place away from Dadaab. They confirmed what we already knew: Al-Shabaab militants were mixing with the refugees coming from Somalia to the refugee camps.

The next few days around the base camp were pretty glum. We had to shut down all operations outside of Dadaab until we could develop a feasible security plan to keep our employees safe. Morale was beginning to decline, everybody was on edge, and we were tired of the camel, rice, and beans served every meal since arriving. We asked the cook if she could go out and find some chicken for a change. She obliged us by showing up with a tiny hen that looked like it was suffering from malnutrition. She prepared it by boiling it, but there wasn't enough meat to serve two people, so it was back to the camel, rice, and beans. I caught myself grumbling about the monotonous diet day after day until one morning, the Lord spoke to me during devotions about my ungrateful heart. I was in the middle of a drought-stricken area where thousands were dying from a lack of food and water.

Yet, I was grumbling about not having the "cucumbers, melons, leeks, onions, and garlic," just like the whiny and unappreciative Israelites.

Americans are the wealthiest people in the world, and instead of gratitude, we are entitled. When I was the special agent in charge of the Secret Service Chicago Field Office, around Christmastime, we helped sponsor an event called Operation Santa Claus. We took up a collection, and some of our agents went out and purchased gifts for children in some of the low-income areas of Chicago. About a week before Christmas, we would throw a party for the kids, and Santa would show up and hand out the presents that had been purchased. Each year, I was disappointed by a few of the children who would receive their gift, look at it with dissatisfaction, and take it back up to the front of the room to rummage through the remaining gifts to find something they might like better. The sadness I felt in witnessing that must, in a small way, be what God feels when we are ungrateful for what He has given us.

I contrast that experience with the numerous Samaritan's Purse Operation Christmas Child shoebox distributions I have been on overseas. The children are seated on the floor and given a shoebox full of very simple toys and gifts. On the count of three, they all tear into their shoeboxes at once. The excitement and squeals of pleasure as they see what is in their boxes are priceless! After the telling of the Christmas story, they all run home, clutching their prized shoeboxes, excited to show and share what they have received with their families. This is the attitude of thankfulness we should all feel about God's blessings, no matter how small, even if it is just camel, rice, and beans.

Father, forgive us when we are ungrateful. Your Word says that every good thing comes from You, whether it be our daily sustenance or possessions. Give us hearts of gratitude and thanksgiving, and open our eyes to how You take care of us daily. Amen.

The Diminutive Saint

For you created my inmost being; you knit me together in my mother's womb. I praise you because I am fearfully and wonderfully made; your works are wonderful, I know that full well.
-Psalm 139:13–14

FEBRUARY 3, 1994, was a bitterly cold day in Washington, D.C. I was working the day shift and arrived at the White House at 5:30 a.m. for the shift briefing going on duty at 6:00. As I looked at the president's schedule for the day, I was glad to see there were several local movements away from the White House. This was always welcomed as the time passed faster when the president was out and about the city. The alternative was "standing post" around the Oval Office for eight hours, which made for a long day.

The first thing on the president's schedule was a 7:00 departure for the National Prayer Breakfast at the Washington Hilton Hotel. We arrived and escorted President and Mrs. Clinton to the Holding Room, where they would stay until it was time for them to go on stage. I took my position outside the door while two other agents entered the room with the Clintons. After a few minutes, the supervisor asked me to step inside the Holding Room and relieve one of the two agents so that he could move to his position next to the stage in the ballroom. As I stepped into the room, I caught my first glimpse of her. She was dressed in her characteristic white habit, trimmed in royal blue. She looked small and frail, especially next to President Clinton. She appeared to be in a passionate, animated, yet respectful conversation with the president. I couldn't hear what she was saying, but as I relieved the other agent, he said, "She's giving the boss hell about abortion." This was my first exposure to Mother Teresa!

At the appointed time, the Clintons moved to the stage, and the program began with the singing of God Bless America and a short address by Vice President Gore. Mother Teresa was introduced, and she stepped from behind the curtain and up to the microphone. Even though they placed a box behind the podium for her to stand on, all that could be seen was the top of her head. Without any opening statement or fanfare, she simply started with a prayer:

> *Make us worthy, Lord, to serve our fellow men throughout the world who live and die in poverty and hunger. Give them through our hands this day their daily bread, and by our understanding love, give peace and joy.*[1]

She then proceeded to speak of loving and caring for our neighbors as Jesus had commanded. She talked of our responsibility for ministering to the poor, the value of families, and other social justice issues that you would expect her to address. Everyone was getting settled comfortably in their seats when she suddenly dropped the bomb:

> *But I feel that the greatest destroyer of peace today is abortion, because Jesus said, if you receive a little child, you receive me. So every abortion is the denial of receiving Jesus, the neglect of receiving Jesus.*[2]

Uneasiness enveloped the ballroom, and there was much shifting in the seats. But she was not through:

> *Abortion is really a war against the child, and I hate the killing of the innocent child, murder by the mother herself. And if we accept that the mother can kill even her own child, how can we tell other people not to kill one another?*[3]

Slowly the applause started on one side of the ballroom and spread to the other. Soon, most people stood and applauded continuously for what seemed like four or five minutes. She then continued:

I have gone to all of the hospitals, clinics, and police stations in Calcutta and begged them, please don't destroy the child. I want the child. Please give me the child. I am willing to accept any child who would be aborted and to give that child to a married couple who will love the child and be loved by the child.[4]

As I stood there listening to the impassioned words of this small, frail lady, I became aware of how callous and twisted we had become as a society. While most abortion advocates will throw out the words rape, incest, and the mother's physical and psychological health as justification for abortion, the vast majority of babies are aborted because they are simply inconvenient.

King David marveled at the miracle of conception and birth when he said, "For you created my inmost being; you knit me together in my mother's womb. I praise you because I am fearfully and wonderfully made; your works are wonderful, I know that full well. My frame was not hidden from you when I was made in the secret place, when I was woven together in the depths of the earth" (Psalm 139:13–15). Yet, in all of David's wonder, he did not fully understand what a miracle we truly are.

Consider that your life began when one cell from your mother was introduced to one cell from your father. Your mother's cell had 23 chromosomes that contained half of her DNA, and your father's had 23 chromosomes with half of his DNA. These two cells merged to become one cell, which was your beginning. The newly matched chromosomes in that cell began forming a brand-new DNA code. If the DNA code created in that one cell were written out, it would be three billion characters of code that describe who God intended you to be: height, weight, hair color, physical characteristics, and mental capabilities. Then that one cell with your very specific DNA began to duplicate itself. At two days, you were four cells; at five days, you were sixteen cells. These cells with your particular DNA continued to multiply until the day you were born when you had approximately 26 billion cells on the way to the 50 trillion cells you would have as an adult. And you are the only one with this unique DNA code that has ever lived or will ever live. If King David had this information, he would have been blown away!

Many of us long to see miracles as the Israelites in the Old Testament experienced, but we fail to recognize the miracle of conception and birth in our world every day. As I was researching the topic, I was surprised to see how many scientists and doctors referred to conception as "a miracle," even though many were not believers. So how could we so brazenly have destroyed over 63 million of God's unique masterpieces made in His image over the past 50 years?

At the same time, I am not condemning those individuals who may be carrying guilt about abortions in the past. The miracle of God's forgiveness is even bigger than the miracle of conception and birth!

In March 1995, I accompanied Mrs. Clinton and her daughter, Chelsea, to India on a three-day visit. Our first stop was Mother Teresa's orphanage in Delhi, which was only one of over a dozen orphanages she had established across India. As I walked in, I was overwhelmed by the number of beautiful dark-haired, dark-eyed children from infants up through six years old. Eighty to ninety percent of them were little girls because the Indian culture often does not value girls as much as they do boys. They were clean and well cared for, and the love the attending nuns gave them was moving. A children's choir was supposed to welcome Mrs. Clinton as she arrived, but a recent spate of adoptions had reduced the choir to just of few school-aged children, a positive sign that the orphanage was serving its purpose. As I strolled around the building observing these beautiful little girls, I couldn't help thinking that each of these children was "fearfully and wonderfully made," each one nothing short of a miracle! No wonder Mother Teresa begged for unwanted children to be brought to her. She didn't see them as an inconvenience; she saw them as masterpieces and valuable gifts from God.

Jesus responded the same way as He chastised His disciples for trying to keep the children away from Him. He didn't see them as an inconvenience but said, "Let the little children come to me, and do not hinder them, for the kingdom of heaven belongs to such as these" (Matthew 19:14). I could imagine Jesus walking into that orphanage in Delhi, picking up one of those young girls, placing her on His lap, and saying, "Therefore, whoever takes the lowly position of this child is the greatest in the kingdom of heaven. And whoever welcomes one such child in my name welcomes me" (Matthew 18:4–5).

Lord, in Your Word, You repeatedly say that we must take on the characteristics of a child, humble, trusting, and forgiving. This tells us that children have a special place in Your heart. We pray that You will constantly remind us of the miracle of conception and birth and that every human life is valuable in your sight. Amen.

The Anonymous Letter

In your anger do not sin: Do not let the sun go down while you are
still angry, and do not give the devil a foothold.
-Ephesians 4:26–27

ANGER IS SOMETHING that we all struggle with from time to time. It is a strong emotion and by far the hardest to control. Its danger is that it causes us to impulsively strike out at the cause of our anger and do things that we would never consider doing any other time.

Paul addresses anger in Ephesians 4:26, but notice that he does not forbid it. He says, "In your anger, do not sin." We are all human, and as long as we are a part of this sinful world, we will experience anger. The Old Testament often talks about God's wrath, and the gospels record Jesus's anger on several occasions. It is not a sin; it is okay for us to feel angry sometimes. Sin comes in when we do not manage it properly, causing us to "give the devil a foothold."

In 1990, I was assigned to the Secret Service office in Shreveport, Louisiana. One morning, an anonymous handwritten threat arrived at the office through the mail with no return address, postmarked Alexandria, Louisiana. The letter stated in part that the "people of Iran" were "declaring war" against the United States. It further avowed that President Bush, former President Reagan, and England Air Force Base in Alexandria were being targeted. There were no leads in the letter other than a statement identifying a certain David Carter as a "comrade." I called the England Air Force Base Office of Special Investigations (OSI) to let them know about the letter and then faxed them a copy. I didn't have much to go on but decided that I would travel to Alexandria the next day to see what I might be able to come up with.

That evening as I watched the news, a report came on that a threat against England Air Force Base had been received and that the base had gone to DEF-CON 4 threat level, meaning tighter security measures. The cameras panned to the front gate, where a long line of vehicles was waiting to be searched before being allowed onto the base. The news reported that it was taking over an hour to gain entrance through the gate in some instances. The reporter stated that security would remain at this level until the Secret Service determined it was all clear. I was surprised first to hear things had spiraled up so quickly and second that England Air Force Base was waiting for me to find the source of the threat letter and let them know when they could resume normal activity. They certainly had more confidence in my investigative abilities than I did! Under the circumstances, I thought it best if I packed my bags and got to Alexandria that evening instead of waiting until the next day.

The next morning, I left my Alexandria hotel and headed to England Air Force Base to meet with Air Force OSI. As the news had reported, a long line of cars was waiting to enter the front gate. I badged my way through the gate and drove to the OSI office, where I explained that I did not have any leads on the origin of the threat other than the name "David Carter" that appeared in the letter. They agreed it wasn't much to go on, but the base commanders thought it best to stay at the current threat level for the week or until there was some resolution.

My first order of business was to try to locate every David Carter in a thirty-mile radius of Alexandria. Through driver's licenses, tax, and utility records, I identified six individuals within the defined area with that name. Over the next two days, I tracked down and interviewed five of them. My initial thought was that one of the David Carters might know someone trying to get him in trouble by planting his name in a threatening letter. Even though I did not consider any of them suspects at that point, I went ahead and got handwriting samples and fingerprints from each of them. Four of the David Carters couldn't think of anyone who held enough grudge against them to implicate them in the threat letter. The fifth said he had some problems with a couple of Middle Eastern men in the past but couldn't give me any identifying information or names. At this point, the investigation was at a dead end. All I could do was overnight the original threat letter along with the fingerprints and handwriting samples to our forensics lab for analysis. I called OSI and let them know I had run out of leads and was heading back to the office to await the results from the lab report.

Several days had passed when I received a call from our forensics lab in Washington, D.C. They had not been able to lift any fingerprints off the letter, and none of the handwriting samples was an exact match. There was only one other test they could run—an indentation analysis. This is where the letter is put through a process to reveal any indentations that might have been left by someone writing on a sheet of paper on top of the paper the threat letter was written on. This was the slimmest of possibilities but our last hope.

The following day, I got an exciting call from the lab technician in Washington, D.C. The indentation analysis revealed some writing from a previous letter written by the suspect. She faxed me an image of the letter that had been developed. At the top of the page was the name "David Carter" with the return address of the last David Carter I had interviewed in Alexandria, along with the full text of a letter to his girlfriend. I excitedly called OSI in Alexandria to let them know we had a suspect and then jumped in my car and headed back to Alexandria.

Upon arriving at David Carter's house, I knocked on the door, and he invited me in. I read him his rights against self-incrimination and then asked him again about his knowledge of the threat. He again denied knowing anything about it, so I took out a copy of the developed letter he had written to his girlfriend and started reading it word for word. He became wide-eyed, and his countenance fell as he sank back onto a chair in his living room. After a moment of total silence, he looked up at me and admitted writing and sending the anonymous threat. I asked him what his motivation was. Again, there was a period of silence, and then, shaking his head, he said, "I was just angry at the world." He had just broken up with his girlfriend, he was having trouble at work, and his father had just recently passed away. His anger had built up inside of him to the point that he felt he needed to lash out at society somehow, and the letter was his way of doing that. He had no prior criminal record, no history of mental illness, and had never considered such an act before. But his unresolved anger had built up inside of him to the point that it had pushed him to the brink.

David's story is a cautionary tale for all of us. Fortunately, he did not take the route some take by resorting to violence in the workplace, school, or at home, but it was a tragedy just the same. He faced the possibility of several years in prison for his actions.

I have to admit that anger has been a problem for me. I remember driving with my youngest daughter one day when a car suddenly forced its way in front of us without signaling. I was still muttering under my breath about the inconsiderate driver when my daughter looked directly at me and asked, "Now, how did that hurt you?" She was absolutely right! My pride and feelings had been hurt, but the actual impact was that I arrived at my destination one second later than I would have if the car had not pulled in front of me. Paul said, "Get rid of all bitterness, rage and anger, brawling and slander, along with every form of malice" (Ephesians 4:31). In other words, choose not to be an angry person. I find that if every morning I resolve with the help of the Holy Spirit to be patient, loving, understanding, and humble, I am much less apt to fly off the handle at some perceived slight or wrong done to me.

Second, we need to be slow to react. James said, "My dear brothers and sisters, take note of this: Everyone should be quick to listen, slow to speak and slow to become angry" (James 1:19). Yes, there is value in the adage to "count to ten" before responding in anger. What is the value of that ten seconds? It allows you to consider the ramifications of your response. Will it ruin a friendship? Will it escalate the situation? Will I soon regret what I am about to say? The Roman poet Horace once said, "Anger is momentary insanity." No decision or response should be made during this short time of irrationality. As I have often said, once a word is spoken, it cannot be unspoken.

Third, Paul says, "Do not let the sun go down while you are still angry." Anger is like a fire. If it is not quickly quenched, it will spread and cause destruction. While camping, we always make sure a campfire is out before we go to bed. If we don't, the results could be catastrophic. The same is true with anger. If we do not quench it quickly, anger can spread and grow into something destructive. This was the case with David Carter. It appeared that he had let his anger fester and grow until he could no longer control it and felt he had no other recourse than to strike out at somebody. Why he did it the way he did is somewhat inconceivable, but again, unchecked anger is insanity.

Father, we pray that You will strengthen our self-control. Our emotions can quickly get away from us and severely hurt our Christian witness. Show us that most of what angers us comes from our uncontrolled pride and egos. Give us calm and peaceful spirits so that we may represent You and Your kingdom well. Amen.

Freedom Rejected

It is for freedom that Christ has set us free. Stand firm, then, and do not let yourselves be burdened again by a yoke of slavery.
–Galatians 5:1

AS HE APPROACHED the front door of the ambassador's house, he walked like a man tired from carrying the world on his shoulders. Two security men accompanied him, and as I held the front door open for them to enter, he stuck out his hand and introduced himself, "Hi, I'm Mikhail Gorbachev." I shook his hand and said, "Yes, sir, we've been expecting you. President Carter is waiting for you inside." I escorted him into the living room where President Carter was waiting and then closed the door as I exited. As we walked back to the front door, the U. S. State Department political officer walking next to me said, "He's the nicest man you will ever meet, but probably the most hated person in Russia."

It was November 1992, and former President Carter was in Moscow for several days of meetings less than a year after the collapse of the Soviet Union. Gorbachev resigned as president on December 25, 1991, and the Russian people blamed him for the superpower's demise, despite his efforts to give them more freedom and deliver them from the strong-armed rule of Lenin, Stalin, Khrushchev, and Brezhnev among others. He had tried to provide them with the freedom to vote, more freedom of religion and speech, and allowed them to keep more of what they produced instead of it all going to the state. He had refused to use military force to quell demonstrations and protests, yet the Russian people had lived for so long under oppression that they did not recognize the value of what he was trying to do for them. When he ran for president again in 1996, he finished seventh with only one-half of one percent of the population voting for him.

The Jews were the same way in Jesus' day. They had lived under the oppression and burden of the law for so long that they knew no other way of life. The constant sacrifices and religious rituals were burdensome, and they lived under overbearing religious statutes and the continuous watch of the religious leaders. Jesus came to offer them an entirely new way of life, free from this oppression under the new covenant, but like the Russian people, they felt more secure in the old way. They were like newly released convicts we hear about from time to time who have been incarcerated for so long that they don't know what to do with their newfound freedom and long for their old life back in prison.

Yet we are guilty of the same thing. We can't let go of the old law and its burdensome work requirements. We live under the pressure of trying to do something to earn our salvation and are always left to wonder if we have done enough. But we have newfound freedom in Christ! We no longer live under a mentality of an oppressive checklist where we have to tick off all the boxes. If we choose to live that way, we will never have total assurance of our salvation. Paul said, "For it is by grace you have been saved, through faith—and this is not from yourselves, it is the gift of God- not by works, so that no one can boast" (Ephesians 2:8–9). This is revolutionary; we have been given a gift! We would never accept a gift from somebody and continually try to pay for it. The idea would be highly offensive to the giver, and if we paid for it, it would no longer be a gift. We could boast about our purchase without giving credit to the person who initially provided it. So why do we continually live under the burden of trying to pay for and earn our free gift of salvation?

Many of us have lived under the adage, "If it seems something is too good to be true, then it probably is." In my experience, this is generally the case. When someone wants to give us something for free, it is usually with strings attached or some fine print somewhere. Maybe this is why we feel the need to do something to earn our salvation. Surely nothing as wonderful as the gift of salvation can be free. We believe there must be some fine print, so we dig up the old law of works to try to earn it, never stopping to realize that while it is free for us, it cost our Lord everything.

But what about when James says that "faith by itself, if it is not accompanied by action, is dead" (James 2:17)? Here he is talking about a faith that involves only head knowledge. This is not real faith. He goes on to say, "You believe that there is one God. Good! Even the demons believe that—and shudder" (James 2:19). In other words, even the demons believe who Jesus is, yet they continue to do the bidding of Satan. True acceptance of God's gift of salvation will result in gratitude so great that there will be a natural outpouring of love and works. Forced works or works of obligation will never lead to salvation, only oppression.

As I walked through the streets of Moscow back in 1992, I was struck by how depressing it was. Part of it was the gloomy weather they had that time of year, but most of it was the lack of hope I saw on the people's faces. Under President Gorbachev, they had been so close to breaking free of the oppressive totalitarian government they had been under for years, but they had rejected him and gone back to what they were familiar with. We have the same choice; we can continue to live under the overbearing pressure of the law and works, or we can live in the freedom that Jesus paid so greatly for us to enjoy.

Father, thank You that we no longer have to carry the burden of our sins because of the price Your son paid for our forgiveness. Forgive our feeble attempts to earn what You have so graciously given out of extreme love for us. Make us ever mindful that we could never do enough to repay the debt that you have absolved. Amen.

Going Through the Motions

———— ✦ ————

"These people honor me with their lips, but their hearts are far from me. They worship me in vain; their teachings are merely human rules."
-Matthew 15:8–9

PRESIDENT CLINTON LOVED to be out among the public. He would see a group of people beside the road waiting to see his motorcade go by and would have the limo stop so that he could get out and shake their hands. It got to the point that we would have a couple agents precede the motorcade by several minutes so that they could be in the crowd, anticipating that President Clinton would probably want to stop and visit with the group.

He was the same way with his morning runs. He enjoyed going out the south gate of the White House to run on the National Mall at 7:00 or 7:30 a.m. when people were on the sidewalks and streets walking to work. That really complicated things for those of us who ran with him. The Secret Service supervisor would run next to the president, along with the military aide and any other guest the president had invited to run with him. The limo and the Secret Service Follow-up would trail at a distance, and four agents would run in a box formation with two agents in front of the president and two trailing him. The two agents in front would engage anyone walking toward us with a friendly greeting such as "good morning" or "how are you doing?" Through this interaction with each individual, we could quickly pick up on signs that might indicate a possible threat. At the same time, if they had their hands in their pockets, we would politely explain that the president was right behind us and ask if they would mind making their hands visible. Ninety-nine percent of the people were highly cooperative and excited to see the president. Every once in a while, we would get someone who was belligerent and uncooperative. The agent would have to stay with that individual until one of the rear agent runners could catch up and remain close to the person until the president had passed and was a distance away. He would then run to catch up.

For President Clinton, it was a rather leisurely run, but for the four agents running with him, it was a real workout with the constant stopping and then sprinting to catch up. We had the system down and operated for months without any issues. I admit that I had gotten a little lackadaisical, as often happens in security work when there are extended periods with no incidents. My priority was getting through the run without having to drop out and rest in front of the White House Press Pool, which was constantly filming the president's movements. The significance of what I was doing had faded into the mundane, but that was about to change.

In early February 1994, we were getting our shift intelligence briefing before going on duty that morning when an agent from the Intelligence Division came in with serious information. Completely unknown to us, toward the end of January, an individual from Florida with a history of mental illness had decided he was going to commit suicide. He got in his car with a loaded handgun and headed to South Carolina, where he planned to shoot himself while standing over his grandparents' graves. However, he missed the exit on the way and found himself almost in North Carolina. Instead of turning around, the subject devised a new plan. He would travel to Washington D.C. and shoot the president! He had seen on the news that President Clinton ran every morning and thought that would be the perfect opportunity. He hoped that in the process of attacking the president, he would be killed.

The subject had checked into a motel in Alexandria, Virginia. Early every morning for several days in a row, he left the motel with a camera bag to catch the metro to the National Mall. There, with his gun in the camera bag, he would wait for the president to run by. Fortunately, and unbeknown to him, the president was traveling that week.

The subject eventually ran out of money, checked out of the motel, and headed back to Florida. When he got home, one of his friends asked him where he had been. When the friend heard that the subject had been to Washington D.C. and what he had planned, he called the Secret Service office in Tampa. Agents were able to piece together the story through the admissions of the subject and the motel clerk in Alexandria, who witnessed him leaving the motel early every morning with the camera bag and returning mid-morning. The clerk remembered him wearing shorts and a windbreaker in the freezing weather. She also recalled him asking her how to get to the Mall "where the president jogs." Hearing this intelligence report from the agent had a sobering effect on all of us on the shift. Would we have been alert enough to stop the assailant?

Later that morning as we ran, I was no longer just going through the motions. My senses were sharpened, and everyone who approached us on the sidewalk that day, in my mind, was a potential attacker. Every thought and action I made had a purpose. I was no longer mindlessly running to complete the task; I was running with a sense of duty.

Many passages in the Bible record God's displeasure with those just going through the motions, but no passage displays his anger more than Isaiah 1:11-15. Israel is still offering sacrifices and incense and keeping the holy days, but God detested their offerings. Why? Because they had turned into a daily ritual without purpose.

"The multitude of your sacrifices—what are they to me?" says the Lord.
"I have more than enough of burnt offerings, of rams and the fat of fattened animals;
I have no pleasure in the blood of bulls and lambs and goats.
When you come to appear before me, who has asked this of you,
this trampling of my courts? Stop bringing meaningless offerings!
Your incense is detestable to me. New Moons, Sabbaths and convocations—
I cannot bear your worthless assemblies. Your New Moon feasts and your appointed festivals I hate with all my being. They have become a burden to me;
I am weary of bearing them. When you spread out your hands in prayer, I hide my eyes from you; even when you offer many prayers, I am not listening.
Your hands are full of blood!

Two statements jumped out at me in this passage that have implications for us today. "I cannot bear your worthless assemblies." They were congregating, but no true worship was taking place. Jesus said the same thing in Matthew 15:8–9 when He said, "These people honor me with their lips, but their hearts are far from me. They worship me in vain; their teachings are merely human rules." That is such an indictment of our churches today! If no true worship takes place, they are "worthless assemblies."

The second disturbing part of this passage is when God says, "When you spread out your hands in prayer, I hide my eyes from you; even when you offer many prayers, I am not listening." Can this be true? Is it possible that He is not listening when we pray even though we are going through all the proper motions? Without a pure heart, yes.

So how do we get out of this cycle of going through the motions? The answer is in verses 16–17, which say, "Wash and make yourselves clean. Take your evil deeds out of my sight; stop doing wrong. Learn to do right; seek justice." In other words, repent and ask forgiveness for your sins every day, take time regularly to draw closer to God, live with an attitude of praise and thanksgiving, and strive persistently to be more Christlike. If you do these things, you will no longer be just going through the motions but have a real purpose. Like the wake-up call I got that morning in the intelligence briefing, your spiritual senses will be sharpened, and your eyes and ears will be opened to God's promptings and the needs around you.

Lord, I pray that You would again instill in us a sense of Your purpose. Our churches and we have become dry and carry on with an attitude of business as usual. I pray You will wake us up and allow us to remember our first love. As Your Word says, You take no pleasure in our legalistic assemblies without purpose. Turn our hearts back to You, we pray. Amen.

The Big Wooden Door

"So I say to you, ask and keep on asking, and it will be given to you; seek and keep on seeking, and you will find; knock and keep on knocking, and the door will be opened to you. For everyone who [a]keeps on asking [persistently], receives; and he who keeps on seeking [persistently], finds; and to him who keeps on knocking [persistently], the door will be opened.
-Luke 11:9–10 AMP

AFTER GRADUATING FROM Howard Payne University in Brownwood, Texas, with a degree in secondary education, I was hired by May High School in May, Texas, to coach their boys' and girls' varsity basketball teams. I had mediocre success and quickly realized that coaching basketball in a Texas high school where football was king was a difficult proposition.

My wife, Jan, and I moved to Mansfield, Texas, the following year, where I accepted the position of junior varsity and assistant varsity basketball coach at Mansfield High School. Mansfield basketball was top-rated, and we were building a successful program, but I began to feel a tugging toward my childhood dream of being an FBI agent. I found myself applying for the position of a special agent with the FBI in Dallas and was invited to take the written test. When the athletic director found out, he advised that I should either drop the application process or resign my position as basketball coach at the end of the 1982 school year. I felt I had no option but to resign and pursue my federal law enforcement dream.

It was a scary feeling walking away from a job with no other means of support in sight. It was especially sobering because Jan and I were expecting our first child in November. I was determined to follow my dream, but I also knew that the hiring time for these federal positions often took over a year. I found a job as an insurance adjuster in the Ft. Worth/Dallas area and settled into applying with as many federal law enforcement agencies as I could. I immersed myself in filling out applications and trying to get my foot in the door to talk with anyone in any agency that might be hiring. Even though I had passed the exam with the FBI, I had not heard anything since, and they were not returning my calls. I applied with the U.S. Marshals, the Customs Service, Immigration, and ATF, but none were hiring or interested in talking with me.

One day as I was leaving the Federal Building in Ft. Worth, disheartened and losing hope, I glanced at the building directory and noticed U.S. Secret Service listed on the sign. This piqued my interest, as I had never considered that agency. I had always assumed that Secret Service agents were all former military or that you had to have some sort of invitation or special skills to be considered for a position. There was a certain mystique about the Secret Service in those days, and the public knew very little about them. I made a note of the floor and suite number and went back upstairs to see if I could find the office. What I found was a big wooden door with no windows and a peephole. I gathered myself and gently knocked on the door. There was no answer, so I knocked again, this time a little louder. Still no response. I must have stood in front of the door for five minutes, pondering what I should do.

Frustration welled up inside me as I thought of all the time I had spent just trying to get my foot in the door to talk with someone. I grasped the doorknob and twisted it. To my surprise, the door was open. I stepped into a small unwelcoming waiting room and faced a large bullet-proof window. A lady was sitting on the other side of the glass. I asked if there was someone I could talk to about applying for a position. She picked up the phone and made a call. A moment later, a gentleman appeared at the front glass, introduced himself as Resident Agent Dave Baldelli, and asked if he could help me. He was a friendly and helpful guy, and after some small talk, he gave me an application packet to take with me. He said I could mail it back to the office addressed to his attention.

As I turned to leave the office, the frustration that I had felt just a few minutes prior had turned into a small beam of hope. Finally, I was able to make personal contact and talk with someone! I resolved that there was no way I would use the postal service for this application process. Every chance I got, I would personally show my face at that big bullet-proof window until they knew me by name.

After completing a rather lengthy application, I showed up again at the big window, hoping to see Agent Baldelli. When I learned he was not there, I handed over my paperwork to the receptionist at the front window and left a bit dismayed.

Not willing to let it rest, I called Agent Baldelli the next day. He assured me that he was in the process of reviewing my application. But after two long weeks of silence, I dressed in my best suit and went back to the Secret Service office. I implied that I just happened to be in the area and was dropping in to check on my application. Agent Baldelli was in the office, and as he saw me standing at the window, he looked at his watch and said, "I have a little free time, so come on in and let's talk."

He interviewed me for a full hour, asking questions about my background, work history, and why I wanted to work for the Secret Service. At the end of the interview, he said he would write up the results and submit my application to the Dallas Field Office for the next steps. He gave me the phone number and address of the Dallas office and said that they would be the ones who would be contacting me from that stage on.

I quickly found the Dallas Field Office and after a couple of weeks, showed up at their door to introduce myself to the agent in charge of applicants. It took 10 or 12 visits to the Dallas and Ft. Worth offices and an entire year before I was finally hired as a Secret Service agent. My thought was that until they told me that I was no longer being considered, I was going to keep showing up and asking.

Jesus tells the parable of the "persistent neighbor" (Luke 11:5–10). The Lord had just finished teaching the disciples, at their request, how to pray by giving them the Lord's Prayer as a model. Now He was teaching them a lesson on praying with persistence.

To put this parable into context, hospitality was important to and strictly observed in that culture. If a visitor showed up at your house and you had no bread for him to eat, it put you in a highly embarrassing and frantic position. It is this desperate situation that drove the man to go to his neighbor's house at midnight to ask for a loaf of bread. The neighbor tells the man to go away because he and his family are already in bed, but he persists because he is in a dire situation. Finally, the neighbor relents and gets up to give him the bread he is asking for, not because of their friendship but because of the man's persistence.

Jesus is trying to teach a point about prayer. He says that when we pray, we need to approach the throne of God with boldness and persistence as someone in a desperate situation. Hebrews 4:16 says, "Let us then approach God's throne of grace with confidence, so that we may receive mercy and find grace to help in our time of need." Boldness does not mean that we come as a demanding or insolent brats. It means that we come confidently to Him as a child would come to his father, knowing that the father will do what is best for him. And like any child, we don't ask just once; we persistently ask.

Unlike the neighbor in the parable, God never tires of hearing requests from His children. As we are persistent in prayer, many things can happen. Our attitude toward the problem and the situation itself may change, God may give us what we are asking for, or God may say no, just as He did when Paul asked that his thorn in the flesh be removed. In the end, you can be assured that your Father heard you, and you have your answer.

I can say that my persistence paid off with the Secret Service. I know this because I received thousands of applications over the 25 years I was with the agency. Every time a persistent applicant contacted me, their application ended up on top of my desk. It forced me to do something with it. Others who never followed up often languished in the applicant file. In the end, the persistent ones always got my attention.

Lord, teach us to pray with persistence. So often, we petition You for help once, don't receive an immediate answer, and run off to try to solve the problem in our strength. How frequently this gets us in trouble. Help us realize that constant prayer aligns us with Your perfect will for our lives and allows us to see how You are directing our paths. Amen.

Defending the Oppressed

Learn to do right; seek justice. Defend the oppressed. Take up the cause of the fatherless; plead the case of the widow.
-Isaiah 1:17

SOME SAY THAT Jimmy Carter did not accomplish much as president. While his crowning achievement was the Camp David Peace Accords between Egypt and Israel, he was hamstrung by a poor economy, high interest rates, and a worldwide energy shortage. On top of all this, the Iranian Hostage Crisis, which lasted 444 days at the end of his term in office, overshadowed everything else. Most presidents leave office and fade off into the sunset, adjusting back to private life, renewing their hobbies, playing golf, and making appearances from time to time. But President Carter was different. He was obsessed with helping the oppressed and hurting, seeking justice for those who had no voice, and trying to right wrongs. He established the Carter Center in Atlanta and immersed himself in these social causes worldwide.

I was privileged to serve on President and Mrs. Carter's security detail for three years during the early 1990s. Through this assignment, I was exposed to some of the many causes President Carter championed around the world. An assignment on his detail was not highly sought after because, unlike the other former presidents, his travels usually took him to third-world countries where the needs were the greatest.

One such trip landed me in Georgetown, Guyana, where I was sent to prepare for President Carter to come and monitor the 1992 national elections. The country was divided between descendants of servants and slaves from India and African slaves, both of which were brought in by the British during the colonial era. The Afro-Guyanese seized power in 1966 at the time of their national independence and had held power ever since. The Indo-Guyanese, who were the majority, had been shut out of leadership positions within the government and claimed that there had never been any fair elections held in Guyana since the country had gained independence. The Indo-Guyanese leaders had come to President Carter for help, saying Guyana's elections had always been fraudulent. They wanted President Carter to monitor the 1992 elections to ensure they were honest and fair. President Hoyte, the incumbent, objected to President Carter's participation but eventually agreed after public opinion turned against him. We arrived to prepare for President Carter's visit in this deeply divided and highly emotional environment.

The days leading up to the election were relatively calm, and we were able to go about our business of meeting with the U.S. Ambassador and State Department officials at the U.S. Embassy, arranging for police support and motorcade assistance, and checking out all the sites that President Carter would be visiting. President Carter arrived two days before the election and spent that time meeting with members of both parties and seeing some of the polling sites.

On the morning of the election, things still appeared calm, and I became hopeful that the election would go smoothly. About mid-morning, President Carter flew out to observe some polling stations in remote areas of the country. I stayed back at the airport in Georgetown to monitor the situation and stay in contact with our intelligence sources at the U.S. Embassy. President Carter had been gone only a few minutes when I heard reports of developing unrest in the city. About two hours later, I got the report that a mob had attacked the U.S. Ambassador's car but that he had been able to make it back to the embassy safely. I received several messages from the State Department imploring us to get President Carter back to the shelter of the embassy as soon as possible.

Thirty minutes later, President Carter's plane landed. I briefed the Secret Service detail leader and President Carter on what was taking place in Georgetown and delivered the ambassador's strong recommendation that we get to the safety of the embassy. President Carter thought for a moment but then said that he needed to go back to the hotel so that he could make some phone calls and figure out what he needed to do. He was determined to do all he could to ensure that the election continued so that the voices of people who had been oppressed for years could be heard.

We were able to avoid the mobs and rioters on the way back to the hotel, but we could see evidence of the escalating violence, and smoke was thick in the air. As we arrived at the hotel, we got the news that the election center headquarters had been attacked and ransacked by rioters, and the multi-national group counting the election returns had fled for their lives. President Carter still resisted the idea of taking refuge in the U.S. Embassy, so I dispatched two agents to the embassy to get additional weapons and gas masks.

As we were arranging added security measures, the pilots who had flown President Carter to Guyana informed us that they had been given orders to leave Guyana immediately, with or without President Carter. The pilots felt embarrassed about the situation but said they had to follow orders. They had received permission to fly to Trinidad, about an hour away, and stand by in the event we needed them. As I watched the pilots depart the hotel, I got a sinking feeling in my stomach. There went our ride home!

As darkness fell, things didn't seem any calmer. President Carter had been working the phone all afternoon trying to get the election back on track. There would be no election if the election center was not operational. Once again, the longsuffering majority would be subjected to four more years without a voice in government. Finally exasperated, President Carter said he needed to go to the election center headquarters. We told him there was no way we could make it safely to the headquarters building under current conditions but that we would send two agents to recon the situation.

When they got to the building, they radioed back that the mob still had the building surrounded, and we could hear sporadic gunfire in the background. We informed President Carter but assured him that we would continue to monitor the situation and try to find a way to get him to the headquarters building.

About an hour and a half later, the agents at the election headquarters reported that they might have found a way for us to get into the building. There was a single door at the back of the two-story structure just off a small alleyway. The mob was focused on the front of the building, and we might be able to slip in the alleyway door unnoticed. Four agents and President Carter piled into the two Suburbans, and we headed toward the headquarters building, taking back streets and trying to remain as obscure as possible.

As we pulled into the alley, we saw the door at the far end. We quickly breached the door and entered the building, pushing a small group of rioters towards and out the front door as we went. Within ten minutes, we had the building secured with an agent posted at each entrance. The place was a mess, but the telephone lines were still intact. President Carter got on the phone and started calling the election workers, encouraging them to come back to the election center to continue their jobs of counting votes. Slowly the workers trickled back in as the mob in front of the building began dissipating. By midnight, the ballots were again being tabulated.

The next morning, President Carter held a press conference at the hotel. With nearly all the returns in, it appeared that the ruling party, who had been in power since 1966, would lose the election by over fourteen points. Even as the press conference was taking place, we got word that a large crowd who backed the incumbent president had gathered in downtown Georgetown and was marching toward our hotel. We quickly contacted the pilots in Trinidad and told them we were headed to the airport and asked if they could fly in and pick us up. They agreed but said they would only be on the ground long enough for us to load and go quickly. President Carter and all the agents grabbed their bags, loaded into the two Suburbans, and headed for the airport, taking a long alternate route to circumvent the mob. We arrived at the airport just as the aircraft was landing. The pilots left the engines running as we all clambered on board, and off we headed to Puerto Rico to refuel and then fly home.

As we rose above the ocean and headed eastward, I could see the satisfaction on President Carter's face. Without his intervention, the powerless majority would have had to live under an authoritarian government for another four years. In his book *Beyond the White House,* published in 2007, President Carter recounts this experience in Guyana and states, "It was the most personal danger I have felt since leaving the White House."[5] Yet this is what he lived for, taking up causes for the oppressed. Whether it be building houses for the poor in America, trying to eradicate diseases in Africa, or standing up to evil dictators around the world, this was his calling.

Many of us who are more conservative-leaning in our political and social views often have a blind spot in this area of our Christian belief system. We deny that there are people who are oppressed in various ways in our country. We hear much noise from many who feel they are being oppressed, but I think the true victims are those we never hear from. They are the working poor who are often taken advantage of by the wealthy, the single mother working two jobs to try to make ends meet, and young children who fall behind in school and cannot read or write because they have no support from home. We tend to "write off" people who find themselves struggling in life because we feel they have made poor life choices and not worked or studied hard enough. Too many Christians believe there is a Bible verse that says, "God helps those who help themselves."

Isaiah said, "Learn to do right; seek justice. Defend the oppressed. Take up the cause of the fatherless; plead the case of the widow" (Isaiah 1:17). He wrote this at a time when Judah (the Southern Kingdom) was thriving as a nation but had become spiritually bankrupt. They continued to offer sacrifices and go through religious motions, but their hearts were far from God. In this religious environment, God chastised them for failing to stand up for justice and care for the weak and oppressed. Does this sound like many of our churches today?

The fact is, Jesus dealt mainly with the oppressed and the outcasts of society. Consider the woman at the well with her poor life decisions, lepers, and the crippled and blind beggars whom He healed. The first people to hear the angels' announcement of Jesus' birth were the shepherds—people on the bottom rung of society's ladder. Even the apostles were lowly, uneducated men like fishermen and tax collectors with very little standing in the community.

This fact should give us pause. What are we doing to help the oppressed, the poor, and the fatherless? This is what the body of Christ should be doing. Our example ought to be the New Testament Church, which took care of the widows and orphans, and when they saw an injustice, they moved to correct it. If Jesus thought these people were worth his time, shouldn't we?

Lord, help us to see people through Your eyes, to realize that no matter their appearance, standing in the community, or mistakes, You care for and value them just as much as you do us who think we have it all together. Open our eyes to the needs of the powerless, the uneducated, the working poor, and those who struggle every day to make ends meet. Help us to find ways to serve them as You would and as You've commanded us to do. Amen.

The Son

Jesus answered, "I am the way, the truth and the life. No one comes to the Father except through me."
-John 14:6

A PEW POLL in 2018 revealed that over 80 percent of Americans believe in God.[6] A recent poll touted by *Newsweek* showed that 52 percent of Americans thought Jesus was a great teacher but not the Son of God.[7] Not only does our society discount the identity of Jesus, but they are also teaching that there are many ways to God. Oprah Winfrey famously stated, "Well, I am a Christian who believes that there are certainly many more paths to God other than Christianity."[8]

After retiring from the Secret Service in 2010, I was looking for a way to serve or minister with the skills God provided me. I received that opportunity by joining up with Samaritan's Purse in their relief efforts in Haiti after the earthquake in 2010. At their request, I then assisted them in trying to win the release of one of their employees who had been kidnapped in Sudan.

Several days after returning from Sudan, I received a call from Franklin Graham's office in Boone, North Carolina, to see if I would be available to fly to North Carolina to have lunch with Franklin. I had never personally met him, excitedly accepted the invitation, and scheduled a date to travel to Boone.

We had a nice lunch, and Franklin spent the afternoon showing me around Samaritan's Purse and the town of Boone. As he was dropping me off at my hotel that afternoon, he asked if I would like to go with him to the annual barbecue for employees of Samaritan's Purse and the Billy Graham Evangelistic Association. I accepted the invitation, and later that evening, he picked me up and drove us thirty minutes up winding roads to Grandfather Mountain.

When we got there, he said he had reserved a place for me at one of the tables. I followed him to the front of the massive tent erected for the barbecue, where I was shocked to see a very familiar face. It was his father, Dr. Billy Graham! Franklin walked me to the table, introduced me to his father, and seated me beside him. Wow! I had been around many great and influential people throughout my career, but I never dreamed I would ever meet and have dinner with Billy Graham. With his halo of white hair and the aura of God's spiritual blessing on his life, it was like eating ribs with Moses!

Several days later, as I was looking back on that memorable experience, two things came to mind, giving me even more of an understanding of the importance of my relationship with Jesus. First, there was only one way I got to meet Dr. Billy Graham: it was through knowing and having a personal relationship with his son. Without that connection, I could have walked up to Dr. Graham's residence gate, rung the call box, tried to call him directly, or attempted to get an appointment through his office. None of those things would have worked. It was only by knowing the son that I gained access to the father.

Second, because his son ushered me to the table and introduced me to him, Dr. Graham took a particular interest in me personally as we conversed. It was more than a passing wave or a quick handshake. He was interested in my career background, common acquaintances, and my Baptist missionary upbringing.

By now, I'm sure you know where I am going with this. Jesus said, "No one comes to the Father except through me." God is holy and therefore cannot tolerate sin. However, He loves us so much that He provided a way for us to reach Him— through a personal relationship with His Son. Once we have that affiliation, Hebrews 4:16 says that we can come boldly before the throne of God because His Son, the High Priest, has spoken up for us and commended us to the Father.

The world will call us intolerant and narrow-minded. Jesus's own words would agree, for he says, "Enter through the narrow gate. For wide is the gate and broad is the road that leads to destruction, and many enter through it. But small is the gate and narrow the road that leads to life, and only a few find it" (Matthew 7:13–14). Americans have it backward. The majority believe in God, but Jesus is just another way to reach Him. If this were indeed the case, Jesus would have said, "Wide and broad is the gate that leads to life."

Most people are willing to talk freely about their belief in God, but Jesus causes them to squirm. Nothing illustrates this better than when athletes are interviewed after a sporting event. As long as they only want to "thank God," everything is okay, but if they start talking about their personal relationship with Jesus, commentators and networks get nervous and try to end or shift the conversation.

Jesus said that it would be this way: "You will be hated by everyone because of me, but the one who stands firm to the end will be saved" (Matthew 10:22). His pronouncement of being the only way is not popular, but it is truth. Besides, do we really think that God would have sacrificed His one and only Son simply to provide one additional option for us to get to heaven? I think not. He is the only way!

Father, forgive us for devaluing Your son's work on the cross by thinking we can find other ways to You through works, church attendance, or goodness. Your son is the only way to You, despite our attempts to water down the gospel to make it more palatable for the world. Thank You for loving us enough to provide a means of salvation. Amen.

A Soft Answer

A gentle answer turns away wrath, but a harsh word stirs up anger.
-Proverbs 15:1

THREATS AGAINST THE president or vice president and their families were the most critical cases we worked on in the Secret Service. These were referred to as intelligence cases, and we dropped anything else we were doing when one came in. Title 18 United States Code 871 is one of the few laws on the books that, despite our freedom of speech, makes it unlawful to say something. It prohibits anyone from threatening to harm or kill the president or vice president and comes with a maximum penalty of five years and a $250,000 fine. However, unlike other laws investigated by the Secret Service, the goal was not to necessarily make an arrest but to have a tool to determine if the person was a genuine threat to our nation's leaders. Seventy-five percent of threats came from people with mental illness, while the remainder typically came from angry individuals venting through various means, whether it be a drunk patron at a bar on Friday night or someone posting on social media. We took every one of these seriously and made every effort to locate and sit down with that person to try to determine if they indeed had the desire to carry out the threat, and, if so, did they have the background, training, or means to do so. Most of these cases went away quickly once we could talk to and listen to the subject's explanation and dig a little bit into their background to ensure there was nothing adverse there.

I quickly found that the best way to approach these situations was to be upfront and honest with the subject, let them know why I needed to talk with them and ask if they would be willing to speak with me. If I felt the least bit uncomfortable, I would inquire if they had a weapon on them and then ask if they minded if I searched them for my peace of mind. Once we sat down, I would start with some general, non-threatening questions about the incident I was investigating and then let them talk. I only interrupted them every once in a while for clarification on something and to assure them that I was listening while showing as much empathy as possible. Even though their story might take over an hour, by the time they were through, I had a pretty good idea of what was going on in their lives and what had prompted them to make the threatening statements. I did hundreds of these interviews during my career, and though a few of them started adversarially, things usually calmed down by the time we were through talking.

During my entire time with the Secret Service, I only had two intelligence cases in which the subjects were deemed conceivably dangerous to our nation's leaders. One of those cases I inherited from another special agent in the Ft. Worth office in 1985. The subject was a military veteran whom we'll call Henry. Henry had a long history of mental illness. He had threatened the Reagans multiple times and was delusional. He had a recurring dream of someone in a Nancy Reagan mask breaking into his house and terrorizing him. He also tended to travel, which coupled with his military training background, was a cause for concern. We had to know where Henry was all at all times, and when either of the Reagans was in the Ft. Worth region, I had to travel to Wichita Falls in northern Texas to keep him under surveillance 24 hours a day until the Reagans left Texas.

Henry had a somewhat belligerent and violent past resulting in many run-ins with the local police. In fact, the month before I inherited the case, the police had gone to knock on his front door. As the officers approached, they heard a shotgun being racked inside the house, so they retreated, blocked off the street, and tried to get Henry to come out. Their attempts failed, and they eventually had to fire tear gas into the small frame house before he finally exited. Henry was committed to a mental hospital but was released several weeks later.

When it was time for our quarterly visit with Henry, I gave him a call, introduced myself, and asked if I could come by and sit on the front steps of his house and talk with him. He eventually agreed but warned me, "Do not bring the police!" I promised him that it would only be me coming to see him. I certainly did not want to walk up to the front door of a mentally ill individual with a history of violent behavior, so I told him that when I got to his street, I would have someone from my office give him a call, and he could come out and have a seat on the steps. I assured him I would drive up and join him once I saw him sitting there.

I traveled to Wichita Falls, went through what we had agreed to do, and met Henry on his front steps. We sat and talked for a couple of hours; for the most part, he was reasonably lucid. As I was getting ready to leave, he told me that he had something he wanted to show me and motioned for me to follow him to the back of his house. Next to his back steps was a large hole he had dug by hand. He said this would be his fallout shelter because he never wanted to be gassed by the police again. As I was leaving, I gave him my phone number and told him to call me if he had any bad thoughts about the Reagans or if he was planning on traveling anywhere outside Wichita Falls.

By the time I got to the office the next day, I already had a message from Henry. I gave him a callback, and he just wanted to talk for a few minutes. From then on, he started finding an excuse to call two or three times a week. One time, he called to say he was sending me his tax forms because he needed me to do his taxes. Another time, he called to tell me that he had decided to run for president and wanted me to be his campaign manager. Every time he would call, I would put him on speakerphone and just let him talk and listen with one ear while I did some other task.

A couple months later, President Reagan was scheduled to be in Dallas, which meant I would need to go to Wichita Falls and keep an eye on Henry. It was hot in Texas during the summer, so on the way to Wichita Falls, I decided to take Henry to get a hamburger instead of sitting in my hot car down the street from his house. Since we did not have cellphones then, I stopped at a payphone and called him. He was more than happy to take me up on the offer of a hamburger. He met me in his front yard, and we headed down the street to Chili's. We had some interesting conversations during dinner, most of which didn't make much sense, but Henry was content and didn't have that wild look I had previously seen in his eyes. It was only about 7:00 p.m. when we finished with our hamburgers, and I knew I needed to keep an eye on him until 11:00 that night, so I suggested we go to a movie. We finally got back to his house at about 10:30. As he got out of the car, he declared, "I feel you're my friend."

Another year passed, and I eventually got Henry to call me just once a week. There were times when I could tell he was getting off his medications, and I would give his caseworker at the hospital a call, so they could take care of it. He got a new car, and he called to provide me with the new license plate number. Every time he left the city limits of Wichita Falls, he called to let me know. Unfortunately, they found some spots on Henry's lungs the following year, and he eventually succumbed to cancer, but Henry had taught me a lesson I would never forget. As violent and angry as he had been in his past, a soft, gentle voice was like medicine to his troubled soul.

The writer of Proverbs said, "The words of the reckless pierce like swords" (Proverbs 12:18). We've all been there; one wrong word can destroy years of friendship. Every day in the news, we see how one word spoken in anger escalates into an incident, and history is filled with stories of wars and conflicts started by ill-advised words spoken by egotistical leaders. Most of these incidents are filled with regrets. The Bible is full of lessons on taming the tongue because it can be so destructive. The simple fact about words is that they cannot be unspoken once they are spoken. But the writer goes on to say that "the tongue of the wise brings healing." That is what we as followers of Christ are to be—healers.

Today's world is full of so-called believers yelling the truth in anger. But that tactic is not our calling. We are to speak the truth, but with a soft, calm voice. Otherwise, we have two sides yelling at each other, and never in the history of man has that been productive. I love the analogy in the book of James of the bridled horse and the taming of the tongue. He says, "When we put bits into the mouths of horses to make them obey us, we can turn the whole animal" (James 3:3). The horse is a large, powerful animal, yet he is power under control with the bit in his mouth. He is wild and uncontrollable without his submission to this small metal piece that fits over his tongue. So it is with us. If we can bring our tongues under control, we can be a powerful force for the Kingdom.

I once had a lady in my church in Shreveport, Louisiana, who referred to me as "the gentle giant" because of my physical size. It is the biggest compliment anyone has ever paid me, and I have always tried to live up to it. I want to be power under control, but that can only be done with a bridled tongue.

Lord, soothe our angry spirits. When we are tempted to lash out at friends, family, or even strangers, quickly impress on us the consequences of what we are about to say, for spoken words cannot be undone. Please help us be quick to listen, slow to speak, and slow to anger. Amen.

That Darn Cat!

---------------------- ✦ ----------------------

Other seed fell among thorns, which grew up with it and choked the plants.
-Luke 8:7

THE LAST DAY of my White House assignment in 1996 was memorable. At that time, the Secret Service presidential detail was small enough to allow President Clinton to welcome agents and their families into the Oval Office on their final day for a photo-op. He thanked the agents for their service and met and talked with the families.

My two young daughters, Jennifer and Rachel, were in seventh and fifth grade at the time of my departure from the White House. Jan and I had pumped up this occasion to them: they had an appointment to meet the president of the United States!

We arrived about 30 minutes early and went to the Roosevelt Room directly across the hallway from the Oval Office in the West Wing to await our appointment. I gave my daughters a brief tour of the Roosevelt Room, showing them different artifacts placed there by different presidents down through the years and explaining that it was the president's office before the Oval Office was built in the early 1900s. Eventually, the president's secretary came into the room and said that the president was ready to see us and escorted us across the hall and into the Oval Office.

Standing in front of his desk was President Clinton, waiting to receive us. The president introduced himself to Jan and the two girls, asked them a little about themselves and made them feel welcome and comfortable. The White House photographer took quite a few photos of the interaction between the president and us, and as it was time to go, we all posed in front of the president's desk for one last

71

photo. The president was scheduled to depart on an out-of-town trip right after our appointment, and while we were in the office, Marine One had landed on the South Lawn for him. As we were saying our goodbyes, the president invited the girls to watch the departure of Marine One from the South Lawn. He ducked out the door behind his desk and headed toward the helicopter. At the same time, we all left the way we had come in, walked down the hallway, and exited the West Wing onto the Colonnade, which runs the perimeter of the Rose Garden. We were headed out to the South Lawn to watch the president depart when the girls caught sight of Socks, the president's cat, tethered out in the middle of the Rose Garden, enjoying the warm sunshine. They were immediately mesmerized and wanted to pet it. I said no but then relented and allowed them to go. The girls petted him, picked him up, played with him, and took pictures with him, all while the president of the United States waved, boarded Marine One, and took off in the background, completely unnoticed by my two daughters!

On the drive home, Jennifer and Rachel talked about how cool it was to play with Socks. Every time I tried to redirect the conversation back to what an honor it was for them to meet President Clinton—something they would remember for the rest of their lives—the conversation always returned to Socks. Needless to say, their photos with Socks were quickly developed and hung on the wall.

While we laughed and chalked it up to kids being easily distracted by lesser things, a profound lesson can be learned here. It is not that my daughters consciously focused all their attention on something less important. It is that their focus on the wrong thing became so strong that they lost all perspective of what was significant. They were excited about the meeting with the president . . . but then they saw the cat!

We too have problems being distracted from the crucial things in our lives, and Jesus warned us of these distractions. Luke 10:38–42 is the story of Jesus coming to the home of Mary and Martha:

> As Jesus and his disciples were on their way, he came to a village where a woman named Martha opened her home to him. She had a sister called Mary, who sat at the Lord's feet listening to what he said. But Martha was distracted by all the preparations that had to be made. She came to him and asked, 'Lord, don't you care that my sister has left me to do the work by myself? Tell her to help me!' 'Martha, Martha,' the Lord answered, 'you are worried and upset about many things, but few

things are needed—or indeed only one. Mary has chosen what is better, and it will not be taken away from her.'

Mary and Martha appear several times in stories throughout the New Testament. Just from these few stories, we can develop a pretty good picture of their personalities. Mary's actions were always driven by her heart. She anoints Jesus's feet, sits under His teaching, or in the case of her brother Lazarus's death, weeps. On the other hand, Martha was the older sister with the practical "get it done" personality. Nothing would keep her from her work and ensuring the household was run effectively. Most of us with Type A personalities can identify with Martha. We take the lead in our homes, and ultimately, it is our responsibility to make sure things get done. We understand Martha's frustration with Mary for not "helping out around the house," but Jesus's response probably surprised her. He made her see that her priorities were out of order. I can see Jesus shaking his head as He called her name twice. My translation would say, "Martha, Martha, you are worried about things that don't matter. Come sit next to Mary and enjoy My company."

This is the distraction that convicts me the most. My job, my career, everything had to be in order, and I couldn't enjoy the moment worrying about what came next. I missed years of not having an intimate relationship with God because I thought that once I had things under control, I could focus my attention on my relationship with God. The funny thing is that time never came because there was always something else.

The second distraction Jesus warned us about was materialism. Luke 18:18–23 says,

A certain ruler asked him, "Good teacher, what must I do to inherit eternal life?" "Why do you call me good?" Jesus answered. "No one is good—except God alone. You know the commandments: 'You shall not commit adultery, you shall not murder, you shall not steal, you shall not give false testimony, honor your father and mother'" "All these I have kept since I was a boy," he said. When Jesus heard this, he said to him, "You still lack one thing. Sell everything you have and give to the poor, and you will have treasure in heaven. Then come, follow me." When he heard this, he became very sad, because he was very wealthy.

Jesus had no problem with wealth. After all, Job, Abraham, and Solomon were all wealthy and blessed by God, and throughout the Old Testament, wealth was a sign of God's blessing. So why did Jesus have a problem with the rich young ruler being wealthy? Jesus looked into the young man's soul and saw that his wealth was a distraction. He was doing everything else correctly—keeping the law, attending church, and reading his Bible. But wealth kept him from being a fully devoted follower of Christ. I know many wealthy people who use their resources for God's Kingdom. I believe God approves of their wealth and will continue to bless these people financially or in other ways. On the other hand, I know those who call themselves Christians but are miserly with their wealth. Jesus would probably tell them the same thing he told the rich young ruler.

The third distraction Jesus discusses is found in His parable of the seeds and the four soils. When describing the third kind of soil the seed fell in, Jesus said, "Other seed fell among thorns, which grew up with it and choked the plants" (Luke 8:7). Jesus explains that these seeds stand for those who hear and believe but are eventually choked by life's worries and the constant uproar that surrounds and distracts us.

We live in a noisy world. Gone are the days when we could sit on the back porch, listen to the crickets chirp, and just think. Instead, we have streaming services, a smartphone that we stare at for hours on end, news and social media that bombard us constantly with information, and technology that allows us instant communication with anyone around the world. All this noise is the weeds Jesus was referring to. The things that distract and overwhelm us. If we don't partition off some weed-free time with God and His Word every day, we will soon be choked out by the cares of the world. This means just you, the Bible, and the Lord; no television, no smartphone, no internet. As we commit ourselves to this time every day, we will soon find that the ground around us is less overgrown with weeds and our roots are growing ever deeper into the nourishing soil.

Lord, keep us grounded in You and not the things of this world. Whether it be work, entertainment, or materialism, we are so easily distracted from that which matters. Forgive us when we chase after every alluring and shiny thing that comes along, for we have become like little children with short attention spans. We pray that You will draw us back to You and rearrange our priorities to the order they should be. Amen.

Operation Dreamlift

———— ✦ ————

*In everything I did, I showed you that by this kind of hard work we
must help the weak, remembering the words the Lord Jesus himself
said: 'It is more blessed to give than to receive.'"*
-Acts 20:35

MORALE WAS LOW in the Secret Service Chicago field office. It was fall 2007,
and we were coming up on what would be a hectic election year in 2008. Typically, candidates are entitled to Secret Service protection starting in January of the
election year with the approval of House and Senate leadership. This time around,
Congress felt that candidate Barack Obama was at higher risk than previous candidates and mandated protection for him early in 2007. A significant portion of
the responsibility for the security of Senator Obama and his family fell on the
Chicago field office. Agents had to work long hours and weekends with this added protection responsibility, plus keep up with their regular casework. They were
tired and rightfully grumpy.

In October, I received a call from the Sunshine Foundation, a non-profit that
tries to fulfill the dreams of physically challenged and chronically or seriously ill
children between the ages of three and eighteen. They were doing an *Operation
Dreamlift* from Chicago, where they would charter an aircraft and take about a
hundred of these children to Disney World for the day. They needed some strong
backs to help load the kids and their wheelchairs on the plane early in the morning, fly to Orlando and unload them onto a bus for their ride to Disney World.
At the end of the day, the children needed to be loaded back on the plane for
their flight back to Chicago. Fully aware of how busy we were, I still thought this

would be a great organization to support, so I put the word out to see who would be interested. To my surprise, 15 to 20 agents signed up to help.

On the day of the trip, all the agents arrived at the airport before sunrise, and we made our way to the departure gate. Waiting expectantly for us in the departure area were the kids with their nurses and parents in line to get on the flight. The majority of the children were in wheelchairs or special strollers. Many had lost their hair because of their cancer treatments. Some did not appear to be aware of what was happening; others wore big smiles. I watched amazed as agents with their tough-guy personas tenderly lifted the children one by one and carried them onto the plane, found them a seat, and got them settled in. It took us almost an hour before we were finally loaded with the wheelchairs and strollers secured in the baggage compartment.

When we arrived in Orlando, we reversed the process, carrying the children down the plane's steps and loading them onto the waiting buses for the ride to Disney World. At the park, Disney World had people to assist, and the agents were free to enjoy the park until 6:00 when they'd have to reload the children back onto the bus to go home. To my great surprise, most of the agents decided to stay with the kids in the park, pushing them around and assisting them in and out of the rides. It was a long, hard day, but I could feel a sense of satisfaction among the agents as we slowly headed back to our cars in the Chicago parking lot that night.

Over the next several days, I saw a real difference in their attitudes. They were more upbeat and enthusiastic despite returning to the same challenging environment they had left. Several of them even came to me and said they wanted to make this an annual event because it had been life-changing. They had experienced what Jesus meant when he said, "It is more blessed to give than receive" (Acts 20:35).

This simple quote from our Savior has turned out to be a proven medical fact. I have been a runner for my entire career. I don't necessarily do it because I love running but because I love its effect on me. Once I'm well into my run, I can feel the stress melt away. My problems don't seem as overwhelming. By the end of my run, I typically have a completely different outlook on life. It's called a "runner's high." This euphoria is caused by endorphins.

Researchers have now coined a new term: "helpers high." They came up with the term when they discovered that giving to or helping others produces the same endorphins as a good hard run, laughter, or any other pleasurable experience. On top of that, these same researchers say that people heavily involved in giving to and serving others are typically less depressed, have lower anxiety, and have a more positive outlook on life. Our Creator knew exactly what He was talking about when He said we would be blessed when we gave. He wired us that way!

But Christians must distinguish between *self-service* and *true service*. We see many celebrities involved in causes for the underprivileged or victims of social injustice. What is their motivation? They get that helper's high plus the praise of men. Jesus's said, "So when you give to the needy, do not announce it with trumpets, as the hypocrites do in the synagogues and on the streets, to be honored by others. Truly I tell you, they have received their reward in full. But when you give to the needy, do not let your left hand know what your right hand is doing, so that your giving may be in secret. Then your Father, who sees what is done in secret, will reward you" (Matthew 6:2–4). The motivation behind true service is seeing a need and acting on it, not because of the show but because of the Father's love flowing through you. Yes, you will experience that helper's high, but more exhilarating than that, Jesus said you will be rewarded by your Father.

———————————

Father, I pray that You will open our eyes to the needs around us. We go through day after day with blinders choosing not to see because we don't want to be bothered. Serving others can sometimes be messy and inconvenient, but it is what You have commanded us to do. May we follow the example You set when walking on this earth. Amen.

———————————

November 22, 1963

Brothers and sisters, I do not consider myself yet to have taken hold of it. But one thing I do: Forgetting what is behind and straining toward what is ahead, I press on toward the goal to win the prize for which God has called me heavenward in Christ Jesus.
-Philippians 3:13–14

I MET WIN Lawson in 2012 while working for the Billy Graham Evangelistic Association and Samaritan's Purse. Like me, he was a retired Secret Service agent who had worked for Billy Graham and his son, Franklin Graham, after leaving the Secret Service. In fact, he was one of the first security men that Billy Graham ever hired. Win was quite a bit older than I was, having served during the Eisenhower, Kennedy, and Johnson administrations.

If you are a history buff, you may recognize Win's name. He was the lead advance agent for President Kennedy's trip to Dallas, Texas, on that ill-fated day, November 22, 1963. It was a terrible day for all of America, but nobody felt the impact of that day the way Win did. In his own words, he is the only Secret Service lead advance agent ever to lose a president.

Win was an extremely meticulous individual and had the reputation in the Secret Service of being one of the most thorough and best advance agents. Yet, he lived the rest of his life regretting that he had not done something to prevent that national tragedy. The conspiracy theories and "Monday morning quarterbacks" in the media weighed on him constantly throughout his lifetime.

As Win was putting together the advance in Dallas leading up to the tragic day, he had been caught up in the challenging position that every Secret Service advance agent runs into; balancing security concerns against the president and his staff wanting him to be as close and accessible to the adoring public as possible. Several tactics could have prevented the tragedy that day. The president could have agreed to ride with the convertible top up since they were going through areas with line-of-sight issues from tall buildings in downtown Dallas. They could have found a less crowded motorcade route with fewer chokepoints where the limo would have been able to travel at a constant rate of speed. At the very least, since they were traveling slowly through massive crowds, agents could have been riding on the limousine running boards, providing some physical cover for the Kennedys. Win knew all of this, but his hands were tied without specific threat intelligence information. The president wanted to be as close and accessible to his admiring constituents as possible. There was nothing else Win could do, but that didn't ease the sleepless nights and regrets. Having to help load President Kennedy's lifeless body onto the gurney and wheel him into the emergency room at Parkland Hospital remained ever etched in his memory.

But Win Lawson did not let the tragedy in Dallas paralyze or define him. Once President Kennedy's casket had been loaded onto Air Force One at Love Field for the journey back to Washington, D.C., he headed back into Dallas to do what he could with the ensuing investigation into the assassination. Remarkably, a couple days later, he received a call from Secret Service headquarters that he need-ed to return to Washington, D.C., to work President Kennedy's funeral.

As expected, Win was eventually a key witness in the Warren Commission investigation into the Kennedy assassination. For days, he had to relive the tragedy and explain why he did this or didn't do that. Yet he never let his regrets over what might have been, destroy him. He used this tragic experience to influence needed changes in the Secret Service to try to ensure there would never be another event like what he lived through. He continued to rise through the ranks of the Secret Service, retiring in 1981 as a deputy assistant director.

I think I am safe in saying that no person other than Jesus Christ has ever walked this earth without suffering regrets. There may be regrets from wrongdo-ing, mistakes, or like Win, regrets over things they didn't have much control over. None of us are immune to these life-changing events because none of us can see into the future. If we could, mistakes could always be avoided.

Regrets can be debilitating. Consider the regrets the Apostle Paul had. In the name of serving God, he had Christ-followers imprisoned and beaten, and stoned to death. His regrets were deep, with some believing that his "thorn in the flesh"

(2 Corinthians 12:7–9) was the memories and regrets of his actions before his conversion. Oh, the sleepless nights and sorrow he must have endured. That is the context in which he wrote Philippians 3:13–14. He said he had to "forget what was behind and strain towards what is ahead." He overcame his regrets by pressing on toward the goal and calling God had set before him. I fully believe that this is what drove him. He used his past to motivate him to be the greatest missionary this world has known.

Even modern psychologists agree with Paul's wise words. A recent *Psychology Today* article on overcoming regret stated, "Since we can't change the past, we can focus on transforming the present moment and positively impacting the future."[9] Or, as Paul stated, "But one thing I do: Forgetting what is behind and straining toward what is ahead, I press on toward the goal to win the prize for which God has called me heavenward in Christ Jesus."

Lord, we struggle against holding on to the past. Help us to see that regrets left unchecked will rob us of our joy in You. May we trust Your forgiveness for our mistakes and realize that You have separated those sins from us as far as the east is from the west, and it shows our lack of faith when we continue to bring them up before You. Amen.

Truth's Foundation

For the word of God is alive and active. Sharper than any double-edged sword, it penetrates even to dividing soul and spirit, joints and marrow; it judges the thoughts and attitudes of the heart.
-Hebrews 4:12

TRUTH IS STRANGER than fiction, Lord Byron said in his poem *Don Juan*. We often hear the phrase used when someone is trying to convince us that some crazy story is actually true. Being a history buff, I have always enjoyed the quirky side stories that often accompany historical accounts. For instance, Napoleon was once attacked by a horde of rabbits while he was on a rabbit hunt. Apparently, his staff had populated the area with rabbits so that their boss would be successful in his hunt. Unfortunately, these were domesticated rabbits, and they charged at Napoleon, thinking he was there to feed them. They began crawling up his boots and pants, and eventually, he had to escape the bunnies by crawling back into his carriage. President Abraham Lincoln was an accomplished wrestler and found himself in the National Wrestling Hall of Fame in Stillwater, Oklahoma. In his twelve years of wrestling, he reportedly won 300 matches and lost only once. Presidents George Washington and William Taft were also grapplers, but not on the same level as Lincoln.

Unfortunately, in today's news media, social media, and books, the truth is no longer exciting or "strange" enough. It must be embellished or wholly fabricated to compete in the information age.

My first eye-opening experience with this shading of the truth was in the mid-1990s when a book came out regarding the Clintons' behavior in the White House. It was written by a former FBI agent assigned to the White House complex for a few years during the Clinton Administration, and it ended up on the *New York Times* Bestseller List. I took a genuine interest in the book because this agent was at the White House during the same time I was. I was shocked when I read it. There wasn't enough truth in the book for it to be anything but fiction! The same thing happened in 2016 when a former Secret Service uniform division officer released a book regarding the Clintons. Once again, it ended up on the *New York Times* Bestseller List while the author made his rounds on all the talk shows. There wasn't much truth in the book, yet people ate it up, and the opposing political party quoted the book extensively during the campaign. I can say from personal experience that neither of these two authors would have ever been in the position to witness what they claimed in their books. I can only assume that tell-all books about the Bushes, Obamas, and Trumps probably fall into the same category. I am not a political supporter of the Clintons, but I am an advocate for truth.

There is only one source of absolute truth in today's world: God's Word. Everything that Christians believe today must survive the scrutiny of His Word. Hebrews says that the Word of God is "alive and active." It is not an old passe, irrelevant book but a foundational rock that is the same yesterday, today, and forever. Want to know how to raise your children? Don't go to blogs and social media for advice; search the Bible. Want to have the perfect marriage? Don't ask Dr. Phil; search the Bible. Want advice on how to deal with your enemies? Don't look for legal help; search the Bible.

The second part of Hebrews 4:12 says that God's Word is "sharper than any double-edged sword, it penetrates even to dividing soul and spirit, joints and marrow." The truth hurts is accurate when we take God's Word to heart. When we sincerely read the Bible, it is very convicting. We quickly find that we are far from God's standards of holiness. Wherever we find that our lives are inconsistent with God's Word, we must confess and change.

I had a pastor in Shreveport, Louisiana, named Billy Crosby. Before every sermon, he had the congregation repeat these words while holding up his Bible: "I believe the Bible is the Word of God. Every word of it is true. I will receive it gladly. Where what the Bible says differs from my thinking and practice, with God's help, I will change." I love this creed! It is something we should recite every day before digging into God's Word.

The last part of Hebrews 4:12 hits all of us hard. God's Word "judges the thoughts and attitudes of the heart." The truth is that most of us are addicted to drama. We've chosen a side, and that choice determines the news networks we watch, podcasts we listen to, social media accounts we follow, and books and magazines we read. We must accept that most of these sources will put out whatever information supports their agenda, even though it may not be completely accurate. They do this knowing it will elicit strong emotions from readers, resulting in higher ratings and more money for them. We can easily get caught up in their rhetoric, which severely affects our hearts. If we find that the attitudes of our hearts include hate, anger, and bitterness, we're going to the wrong source for truth.

Father, thank You for Your true and unchanging word. May we realize its value in our lives for answers and correction. Forgive us for getting caught up in the rhetoric of this world and placing more credence in what we hear and read over the truth of Your word. Please help us to constantly search the Scriptures for Your truth and make the needed corrections when our lives conflict with what Your word says. Amen.

Strangers in the Land

———— ✦ ————

"When a foreigner resides among you in your land, do not mistreat them. The foreigner residing among you must be treated as your native-born. Love them as yourself, for you were foreigners in Egypt. I am the Lord your God."
-Leviticus 19:33–34

WE HAD 22 federal arrest warrants for gang members who were producing false documents. Several of the gang leaders had recently murdered a competitor in Mexico and had a contract out on a second rival. They catered primarily to illegal aliens in the Chicago area, and their lucrative business was bringing in two to three million dollars per year through their illicit activities. For $200–300, they could furnish you with a set of documents that included a social security card and an immigration "green card" or state driver's license in the name of your choosing.

Immigration and Customs Enforcement (ICE) headed up the investigation called Operation Paper Tiger, but the Secret Service and the FBI assisted in the three-year investigation. We knew the gang operated out of Chicago's Little Village Discount Mall in the Latino section of the city. Even though we had photos of all the suspects, we could not be sure who they were because they tended to operate under various names and identities. For this reason, we needed to catch them in the act where they were operating, and it required us to surround and hit the mall in the middle of the day.

I observed as agents quickly and quietly surrounded the complex and locked down the mall so no one could come or go. The plan worked flawlessly. Within minutes, the facility's outer perimeter was secured, and we were going door to door, rounding up the suspects.

At the time of the operation, about 150 shoppers and workers were present, and all had to be detained until the suspects could be sorted out and identified. The word that an immigration raid had taken place at the mall quickly spread through the neighborhood, and a crowd of 300 protesters appeared out of nowhere, carrying signs, chanting, and shutting down the streets. We tried to convince the protest leaders that this was not an immigration raid but that we had 22 specific arrest warrants. Still, they refused to listen until the doors opened and shoppers, many of whom were in the country illegally, began to exit the building.

As I headed home from the chaotic scene, my thoughts were, "So what if it had been an immigration raid? Most of those people are here illegally!" My mentality was from the perspective of law enforcement, and the rule of law was important to me. I could not understand why many didn't think it was a problem for foreign nationals to show up in our country and blatantly ignore our laws.

After I retired from the Secret Service in 2008, I went to work for a short time with the Internal Affairs Division of Customs and Border Protection. In this position, I often traveled to the southern border to do background investigations and interview border patrol personnel. What I witnessed in the immigration lockups and holding facilities began to somewhat soften my views toward illegal immigrants. The majority of those people who had been caught trying to cross our border were humble, compliant, and not demanding. On the other hand, unlike what the press would have you believe, the border patrol agents treated them with respect, and I never witnessed any abuse, even though they were overworked and in a challenging profession.

Our country is locked in a never-ending debate regarding immigration. One side wants walls and fences with minimal immigration; the other wants open borders with everyone free to come and go. So, what should be the Christ-follower's perspective be on this challenging issue?

Several years ago, we had a significant hail storm in our community, resulting in every house needing a roof replaced. Our street was teaming with roofing contractors, but I noticed that all the roofing crews were made up of Latinos. They would start at 7:00 in the morning and work until the sun went down that evening, taking only a one- or two-hour break in the middle of the day. I was amazed at what they could accomplish on those steep, hot roofs in the middle of the Mississippi summer. When they came to roof our house, I greeted them and invited them to use our back porch to cool off while my wife, Jan, made them a batch of chocolate chip cookies every afternoon. Once the roofers got comfortable with us, their wives, who brought them lunch daily, would come around and sit on the back porch while they ate. At the end of the day, the wives would return with their children, who would run and play in the backyard until their fathers were ready to go.

As I watched these families, not knowing their legal status in the country, I thought back to my German great-grandfather, who had immigrated to the United States, entering the country through Galveston, Texas. He was a dirt farmer who barely eked out a living but had the same work ethic and family values as these Latino roofers. His values were passed down through his sons and grandsons, making me who I am today.

I took a genuine interest in these Hispanic families and found that many of them lived inconspicuously in a small community ten miles northeast of where I lived. It just so happened that about that time, our church opened a Connect Center in that low-income community to tutor and teach English as a Second Language (ESL). My wife and I volunteered to teach English on Tuesday nights, and I started with four or five young Latino men who could speak very little English. I was amazed at the fortitude of these young men who would labor in construction and lawn maintenance all day and then show up that evening eager to learn English. We started out teaching construction terms and then moved to the parking lot to teach car and pickup truck parts and nomenclature. I never asked about their status in the country, nor did I want to know.

One of these young men (we will call him Reyes) was from a country in Central America. He picked up English very quickly, and pretty soon, we would meet every week to speak English for an hour. Reyes opened up, told me his life story, and even detailed the treacherous journey which almost cost him his life on two occasions from his home country to the United States. He spoke lovingly of the two young sons he had left back home and how they loved to play baseball. I asked him about his future plans, and he said that he wanted to stay in the United States just long enough to make sufficient money to build his family a small two-room cinder block house, and then he wanted to return to his country. I asked Reyes what he would do when he got back home, and he told me he would probably go back to rolling cigars for a living. When I questioned how much that paid, he shrugged and said $7.00 daily.

As I think back to the day of the raid in Chicago and my callous attitude toward the people I saw as "illegal occupiers" that we released from the mall, I am reminded that many of them have stories, families they love, and dreams just like Reyes. This makes for a very difficult position politically. While wrestling with the same problem, President Reagan said, "A nation that cannot control its borders is not a nation." I am personally convinced we need to secure our borders for many economic and national security reasons. But I am saying that we as the church need to see all people as individual humans loved by God once they are inside our borders. God told the Israelites, "When a foreigner resides among you in your land, do not mistreat them. The foreigner residing among you must be treated as your native-born. Love them as yourself, for you were foreigners in Egypt. I am the Lord your God" (Leviticus 19:33–34). We must accept that whether they are here legally or illegally, they are probably here to stay. God commands us to "treat them as native-born" and "love them as ourselves."

We have a mission field right in our communities. Our churches are generous in giving money to send the gospel overseas yet overlook the foreigners that have come to us. They are beginning new lives and looking for acceptance in their new community, so who better than the church to reach out and minister to them while sharing the love of Christ.

Father, You have ordained governments to rule and make laws for the good of their citizens and have commanded us to submit to their authority. You have also charged us to love our neighbors as ourselves, and borders do not confine that love. May we always look for ways to serve others in need, no matter their background, race, or nationality, as was so powerfully modeled by Your son. Amen.

Run and Don't Look Back

The prudent see danger and take refuge, but the simple keep going and pay the penalty.
-Proverbs 22:3

WHY IS IT so crucial for believers to flee temptation? After all, temptation itself is not sinning; Jesus was tempted. James aptly answers this question when he says, "But each one is tempted when he is carried away and enticed by his own lust. Then when lust has conceived, it gives birth to sin; and when sin is accomplished, it brings forth death" (James 1:14–15). James says that sin is usually a four-step process. Temptation first, then lust or dwelling on the sin, the sinful act itself, then the consequences. We must look at temptation as a warning sign to "get out immediately." If we linger, we quickly progress to step two, where our chance of resisting is significantly reduced.

If you have done much deer hunting, you know that deer often get spooked either by picking up your scent or hearing a noise. They usually run a short way, then stop and look back. That look back is often their demise! Consider Lot's wife, who, as they were escaping the destruction of Sodom and Gomorrah, looked longingly back at the sinful cities and was turned into a pillar of salt. Temptation works the same way. That lingering second look will too often lure you into sin, followed by its tragic consequences.

The best example in the Bible of someone fleeing temptation is the story of Joseph and Potiphar's wife. Genesis 39:6–12 records the story this way:

Now Joseph was well-built and handsome, and after a while, his master's wife took notice of Joseph and said, "Come to bed with me!" But he refused. "With me in charge," he told her, "my master does not concern himself with anything in the house; everything he owns he has entrusted to my care. No one is greater in this house than I am. My master has withheld nothing from me except you because you are his wife. How then could I do such a wicked thing and sin against God?" And though she spoke to Joseph day after day, he refused to go to bed with her or even be with her.

One day he went into the house to attend to his duties, and none of the household servants was inside. She caught him by his cloak and said, "Come to bed with me!" But he left his cloak in her hand and ran out of the house.

She harassed him constantly, but he refused and avoided her as much as possible. When he was finally caught in an unfortunate set of circumstances, he didn't hesitate for a moment but shed his coat and fled before he even had a chance to consider it or try and justify it.

While not lingering in the presence of temptation is always a good idea, I will take it one step further: don't even go where temptation might lurk. As a young trainee with the Secret Service, I was gone from my young family for about six months—three months in Georgia and three months in Washington, D.C. My training class consisted of men and women in their mid-twenties, half of us were married, and the other half were single. We became a close-knit group, and after a long training day, we would go out to eat together, and then many would head to a bar. I always joined the group for dinner but then excused myself to head back to my room. I figured nothing good could come out of those nights at the bar. I was committed to my family and did not need to put myself in a position of temptation.

Halfway through our training, I was called in for my mid-term evaluation. The advisor told me that I was not coming across as a team player because I had the reputation of disappearing to my room at night and not "partying" with the guys. He further informed me that I would not go far in my career with this behavior. Not exactly an encouraging evaluation!

But I continued the practice throughout my career and retired after 25 years with many close friends. Unfortunately, many of them have gone through several divorces and marriages, largely because of indiscretions on the road. Most of them did not go to bars looking for affairs. It's just that they got there, the temptation was strong, and they did not flee. Many ended up with complicated lives dealing with ex-wives, ex-wives' husbands, estranged children, step-children, alimony, and child support payments. Most of their troubles could have been avoided had they resisted their temptation.

David was a man after God's own heart, but his temptation and sin with Bathsheba cost him years of heartache and sorrow. He was repentant and remorseful, and God forgave his iniquities, but the consequences of his sin followed him for the rest of his life. David's adultery and murder caused tragedy of enormous proportions. The child conceived during his sin with Bathsheba died less than a week after its birth. Amnon, his oldest son who would have inherited the throne, raped his half-sister, Tamar. Absalom, another son, killed Amnon with the sword to avenge what he had done to Tamar. Absalom rebelled against David and was killed by Joab, David's military leader. Adonijah, another son, rebelled against David and ended up being killed by Solomon.

This all started when David was somewhere he should not have been. His men were in the field fighting, and he should have been out on the battlefield with them. Second, when he saw Bathsheba bathing, he did not avert his gaze but instead allowed himself to be enticed. Third, his lust turned to action, and he was suddenly caught firmly in the grasp of sin. All that remained were the years of consequences. He had lost his moral right to lead his family and the nation of Israel. One can only wonder how things would have turned out if he had only been on the battlefield where he was supposed to be or at least fled the temptation after seeing Bathsheba.

After retiring from the Secret Service, I worked for the Billy Graham Evangelistic Association, which holds strict standards for integrity as established by its founder, Billy Graham. These standards were set by Dr. Graham and his team in 1948 with four principles that they followed throughout their lifetimes. The most famous one is known as the "Billy Graham Rule," which deals with the danger of sexual immorality. They pledged to avoid any situation that would give the appearance of impropriety. This meant never traveling, eating, or meeting alone with a woman without others present.

While the "Billy Graham Rule" has been the topic of much debate recently with the "Me Too" movement, there were three other little-known but just as important commitments concerning the handling of money, honesty in publicity and reporting, and working with and not being critical of pastors and local churches. Because of these commitments and pledges, there were never any accusations or appearance of scandal during Billy Graham's 70 years of ministry. Quite remarkable!

Each of us can learn a lesson from the wisdom of Billy Graham. We should sit down, consider where we are weak, recognize where our strongest temptations come from, and resolve to avoid situations where those temptations might be the strongest. It may mean turning off the television, not going to certain places, moving your computer to a public place in your house, and re-evaluating your business ethics. If we don't work to avoid temptation and pre-plan our exit route ahead of time, like King David, we will fall and suffer the dire consequences of sin.

Father, You promise we will not be tempted beyond what we can bear. We ask for Your strength to stand up against temptation every time we encounter it. Open our spiritual eyes to quickly discern the dangerous road we may be going down and give us the strength to flee quickly. Amen.

The Man on the White Horse

The grass withers and the flowers fall, because the breath of the Lord blows on them. Surely the people are grass. The grass withers and the flowers fall, but the word of our God endures forever."
-Isaiah 40:7–8

I WAS IN awe of President Reagan. I'm sure it was because I was still young, inexperienced, and wide-eyed, but I felt it was such an honor to serve him. He made us feel so good about being Americans, and with his calm demeanor and wit, I always felt as if he had things under control and knew exactly the right thing to say at the right time.

Since the Dallas Field Office where I was assigned during the 1980s was considered part of the country's southwest region, I was often called upon to travel to California to help with security when President Reagan vacationed at his ranch in Santa Barbara. Because of my youth, my assignment was "post stander," which meant that I was given a security post in the middle or outer perimeter of the ranch. It was such a long distance from our hotel in Santa Barbara up to the ranch in the mountains that they would have "post standers" work 12-hour shifts each day. We would rotate post assignments every 30 minutes to an hour and take a short break every two or three hours. For the most part, I was standing out in the woods all day—not exactly a glamorous job. As dull as it was, I didn't mind the assignment because, in my mind, I was doing my part to protect the most powerful man in the world!

The highlight of my day was that every afternoon at about the same time, President and Mrs. Reagan would go horseback riding. He would go out and saddle up the horses and then ring a large bell outside the barn to let Mrs. Reagan know that he and the horses were ready to go. As he would come riding by me on his big white horse wearing his brown English riding boots, he would always make a point to smile and speak to me. I could tell Mrs. Reagan was not necessarily enjoying the ride; she was doing it for him. He loved riding that horse, and I felt it was so appropriate that it was a white horse.

The years passed, and President Reagan finished his second term in 1988 and retired to California. He occasionally made public appearances, but he kept his life reasonably private. Then in August of 1994, he revealed to the world in a handwritten letter that he had been diagnosed with Alzheimer's. The letter read:

My fellow Americans,

I have recently been told that I am one of the millions of Americans who will be afflicted with Alzheimer's disease.

Upon learning this news, Nancy and I had to decide whether as private citizens we would keep this a private matter or whether we would make this news known in a public way.

In the past, Nancy suffered from breast cancer and I had cancer surgeries. We found through our open disclosures we were able to raise public awareness. We were happy that as a result, many more people underwent testing. They were treated in the early stages and were able to return to normal, healthy lives.

So now we feel it is important to share it with you. In opening our hearts, we hope this might promote greater awareness of this condition. Perhaps it will encourage a clear understanding of the individuals and families who are affected by it.

At the moment, I feel just fine. I intend to live the remainder of the years God gives me on this earth doing the things I have always done. I will continue to share life's journey with my beloved Nancy and my family. I plan to enjoy the great outdoors and stay in touch with my friends and supporters.

Unfortunately, as Alzheimer's disease progresses, the family often bears a heavy burden. I only wish there was some way I could spare Nancy from this painful experience. When the time comes, I am confident that with your help she will face it with faith and courage.

In closing, let me thank you, the American people, for giving me the great honor of allowing me to serve as your president. When the Lord calls

me home, whenever that may be, I will leave the greatest love for this coun-
try of ours and eternal optimism for its future.

I now begin the journey that will lead me into the sunset of my life. I
know that for America there will always be a bright dawn ahead.
Thank you, my friends.
Sincerely,
Ronald Reagan[10]

When the news broke, it shocked me that President Reagan was suffering from this terrible and incurable disease. I began thinking about how the world typically hangs on the last words of a great man as he is on his deathbed. This would not be the case with President Reagan. With him, the lights would slowly dim until they finally went out.

I was a supervisor in the Los Angeles Field Office stationed at a satellite office in Riverside, California, in 1999. We had assisted the Reagan protective detail numerous times as they traveled to Palm Springs, and I had developed a friendship with the head of the detail. I told him that I would love for my two high school daughters to be able to get a photo with President Reagan sometime. He set it up several times, but we had to cancel because of schedules. Finally, he called me one day and said that if I still wanted to get my daughters a photo with President Reagan, it would need to be the next day. He said, "Tomorrow is probably the last day President Reagan will be going to his office."

The next day, I checked my two daughters out of school, and we drove to President Reagan's office in Los Angeles. We waited in the outer office for a few minutes before President Reagan's secretary ushered us in. There he was, standing in front of his desk, impeccably dressed as always in a dark suit and a red tie, but immediately, I almost regretted I had come. He didn't say anything and seemed somewhat confused, even though he acknowledged us with a slight smile. He shook our hands, but there was no interaction. We took our photos and left the office. As we were walking out, the Detail Leader told me it would probably be one of the last photo ops with President Reagan. Mrs. Reagan, fiercely protective of the president, did not want any more photos taken of him. This was not the man on the white horse I wanted to remember!

President Reagan died on June 5, 2004. His body was flown to Washington, D.C., on June 9, where he was to lie in state in the Capitol Rotunda until June

11. At the time, I was serving as a deputy assistant director and was assigned to be on-site along the funeral processional route on Constitution Avenue. As I watched, the hearse pulled up in view of the south side of the White House, and as per tradition for a presidential funeral, the casket was loaded from the hearse onto the caisson for the procession up Constitution Avenue. Directly behind the caisson was a black riderless horse with President Reagan's English riding boots backward in the stirrups. When I saw those familiar boots, I felt sadness. It was not just the passing of President Reagan; it was the passing of an era that we could never go back to.

Isaiah said, "The grass withers and the flowers fall, because the breath of the Lord blows on them. Surely the people are grass" (Isaiah 40:7). I'm sure when he wrote this, Isaiah was feeling melancholy, wishing for the good old days when his friend, King Uzziah, was alive. King Uzziah was a God-fearing king who had brought the nation back to its greatest days since the reigns of David and Solomon. But Isaiah realized that change is always inevitable. Death is the great equalizer, and leaders are like the rest of us. They wither up like the grass and fade away, along with their accomplishments. Time marches on, new leaders are born, and the country takes a different direction.

On a personal level, as we get older, our health changes, our jobs look different from before, and we have a hard time keeping up with the constant advances in technology. We seem out of control in a changing world where nothing stays the same. No wonder I find myself longing for the 1980s again, a simpler time. But Isaiah's depressing observation ends on a positive note: "But the word of our God stands forever" (Isaiah 40:8).

Science books are updated constantly, history books are revised frequently, and the social sciences come up with new ideas every day, but God's Word is the same today as it was in the 1980s and before. What's more, its truth will continue for millions of years to come. It is the only unchanging anchor we have in this fast-changing world, so read it, study it, meditate on it, and take comfort in knowing there will never be any revisions.

Father, thank You for Your unchanging word. It is a comforting anchor in an ever-changing world. Your truths and promises are everlasting and not constantly shifting with man's whims and obsession with political correctness. Help us to stand firmly on Your word. Amen.

A Hard Lesson

But to you who are listening I say: Love your enemies, do good to those who hate you, bless those who curse you, pray for those who mistreat you.
-Luke 6:27–28

THE LOUD BOOM of a mortar shell several miles away shook the ground and interrupted my thoughts, bringing me back to reality. The beautiful crisp January day in Mosul, Northern Iraq seemed out of sorts with the horrifying setting we were operating in. It was 2017, and Mosul had been under siege by the Coalition Forces for several months in an attempt to retake the city and region from ISIS fighters. Progress had been slow, and casualties were mounting on both sides. However, the real victims of this terrible war were the innocent residents of Mosul who had endured unspeakable horrors during the occupation of ISIS.

Samaritan's Purse felt a real burden for these people and decided to establish a field hospital near Mosul to treat the casualties of the war. No hospitals were operational in Mosul, and the nearest medical facilities were in Erbil, several hours away. Many were dying in ambulances before they could reach those hospitals.

As the Head of Security for Samaritan's Purse, it was ultimately my department's responsibility to put together a security plan for the soft-sided hospital tent city that would house several operating rooms, trauma rooms, ICU, and recovery rooms for patients. We also had to account for the safety of the surgeons, doctors, and nurses who traveled from the United States and other countries to volunteer their services at the hospital.

The security plan involved digging a 10-foot-deep by 10-foot-wide trench around the 20-acre perimeter of the property and installing 10-foot fencing on the inside of the trench to prevent attacks by Vehicle Born Improvised Explosive Devices (VBIEDs). We erected 12-foot-high "blast walls" around the hospital tent compound which was 100 yards inside the fence to protect the hospital tents in the event a VBIED was somehow able to slip through our outer perimeter. The boundaries would be protected by a private Kurdish security force that would reside on the compound.

Our real concern was airspace security because ISIS had started using commercially purchased lightweight drones, retrofitted to carry and drop a three-pound mortar shell. One of these dropped inside the blast walls of our tent hospital would be devastating. We outfitted our Kurdish security force with shotguns loaded with #4 buckshot and instructed them to shoot down any drone flying toward our airspace. Though it was not perfect, this plan would have to suffice until we could find signal-jamming equipment.

We also devised a three-stage security protocol that the ambulances and victims would have to proceed through before they reached the front door of the hospital compound. The process involved three successive checkpoints manned by Iraqi soldiers, explosive technicians, and bomb dogs. We had already been warned by the Iraqi army of a plot they had uncovered of ISIS wanting to steal an ambulance, load it with explosives, and try to gain access to our hospital.

We studied ISIS's methods of operation and their techniques of infiltrating secured areas and tried to address each scenario. There was no doubt in our minds that ISIS was the enemy, and they would like nothing more than to attack and kill western Christians.

The hospital complex was close to completion, and Jamie Gough, Samaritan's Purse Director for International Security, and I had traveled to Mosul to make final adjustments and establish the security protocols for accepting patients. With everything in place, the word was given, and the wounded war victims started pouring in. The ambulances and private vehicles picking up the wounded in Mosul did not distinguish between Iraqi army soldiers, private citizens, or even ISIS fighters. All severely injured were brought to the hospital, where they all received the best treatment possible.

Initially, the staff tended to recoil when they had to treat one of the ISIS fighters, especially after personally witnessing the terrible carnage the fighters had caused. One nurse said that she had to stop and ask God to calm her hatred before going into the area where the injured ISIS fighters were recovering. Another talked about the revulsion she felt one day in the operating room as they frantically worked on a young mother and child who looked like they were going to succumb to their wounds, while an ISIS fighter in the next bed over kept asking for a glass of water.

The medical staff was soon convicted of their contempt for the fighters and realized that they would have to deal with their intense feelings for their own spiritual health. Through constant prayer and Bible study, things began to change. Using interpreters, they began to converse with the young men. They listened to them, heard their stories, and treated them with as much care and respect as possible. The young fighters began to soften, and one was even overheard telling his companion, "These people are not like we were told they would be."

Jesus said, "But to you who are listening I say: Love your enemies, do good to those who hate you, bless those who curse you, pray for those who mistreat you" (Luke 6:27–28). This is without a doubt the hardest lesson Jesus ever taught. I have never heard anyone quote this as their life verse or their favorite passage in the Bible. Even now, as I write these words, I think, "I don't want to love my enemies." This is the case for most of us. While we might never do anything to physically harm those against us, we will undoubtedly take the opportunity to gloat if something bad happens to them.

Jesus modeled this commandment for us throughout his earthly ministry. He reached out to those despised and hated, like the Samaritan woman and tax collectors. He gently healed the ear of one of his captors in the Garden of Gethsemane and later prayed for the forgiveness of those nailing him to the cross. Having been through all of this, he certainly wouldn't accept our feeble excuses.

Jesus knew the destructive nature of hate and bitterness. He knew these unchecked sins continue to grow like cancer and eventually stunt spiritual growth. But just as important, you never know what your overtures may do for your perceived enemy. It may open up avenues of understanding and respect that result in your enemy becoming your brother.

So how are we to start loving our enemies? It is not as simple as just turning our emotions on and off. First, ask the Holy Spirit to soften your anger enough to sincerely allow you to pray for your enemies. I have found it is impossible to honestly and intentionally pray for someone over time and continue to despise them. I am not talking about a short flippant prayer made in passing. I'm talking about daily prayer, not focusing on their evil but on their being made in God's image and loved by Him.

Second, try to empathize. As Jesus was being nailed to the cross, He said, "Father, forgive them, for they do not know what they are doing" (Luke 23:34). He was by no means excusing what they were doing, but he understood why they were doing it. Neither the Roman soldiers nor the Jewish religious leaders knew who He was. To them, He was a criminal and a blasphemer. The nurses serving at the Field Hospital in Mosul could never excuse what the ISIS fighters had done, but they could at least understand that they were fed misinformation. Had the medical staff never listened to their stories and tried to understand, there would never have been any connection between them.

Again, this is a hard lesson that Jesus taught, and it is not something we will be able to accomplish overnight. It will take supernatural help from the Holy Spirit and a willingness on our part to submit. But for our spiritual well-being and our obedience to Christ, it must be done.

Father, we have many blind spots in our Christian walk, but this is one of the most glaring and, by far, the most difficult to overcome. You said even the lost could love their brothers, but it takes Your supernatural help for us to love our enemies. Hate damages our spirits, yet we allow it to grow uncontrolled and seek to justify it. Convict us of this sin and give us the strength to overcome it. Amen.

Family appointment with the President.

Photo with President Reagan in 1998.

Tim coming off Marine One.

Graduation Day photo with Jerry Parr.

Finishing up a run in Shreveport, Louisiana.

Working the rope line in Detroit, Michigan.

Christmas Party with the Carters.

Departing Foundry Methodist with the Clintons.

Socks, the Presidential Cat, with Rachel, and Jennifer.

Riderless horse with President Reagan's boots.

President Reagan's caisson.

Arriving from Camp David

Abba, Father

———— ✦ ————

The Spirit you received does not make you slaves, so that you live in fear again; rather, the Spirit you received brought about your adoption to sonship. And by him we cry, "Abba, Father."
-Romans 8:15

FOR ALMOST TWO years of my total time on the Presidential Detail, I was assigned specifically to Mrs. Clinton. Being a member of the First Lady Detail also meant that I would fill in on daughter Chelsea Clinton's detail from time to time. I actually enjoyed those assignments because it was more laid back without the stress that came from being under the microscope with the higher profile of the president or first lady. We would go with her to school, take her to the mall to hang out, and even accompany her to friends' houses for sleepovers. When it came to dating, I'm sure we were what every father would dream of for their daughter— two armed men driving and watching over their prized possession while she was on a date! Not exactly what a girl would consider ideal, but the young men always behaved themselves! Chelsea was a very polite, friendly, and considerate teenager who took it all in stride.

As Chelsea and one of her friends got into the car after school one afternoon, we asked where she wanted to go. "To the mall to hang out!" she quickly replied. Then she added, "But first, I need to go the house to get my allowance from Dad." We took her directly to the White House, and she jumped out and headed into the West Wing. She emerged a few minutes later with a pleased look, climbed back in the car, and off to the mall we went.

As we got to the mall, we stayed a distance away from Chelsea and her friends to give them some privacy and not draw attention to them; at the same time, we were close enough to respond to any issue or threat that might arise. It was amusing to watch as people recognized her and immediately started looking around to see if they could pick us out of the crowd. It wasn't too hard, considering we were a couple of 35-year-old men trying to dress like and fit in with high school students. They shopped for a while, ate dinner at one of the restaurants, and then we headed back to the White House.

After we got back to the residence, I was writing up the shift report for that day when I realized that Chelsea was like any other teenager in America with the exact wants, desires, and dreams as my two daughters. The only difference was that she happened to be the daughter of the president of the United States. But two things struck me about the events of that afternoon. First, she said she needed to return to the house and get her allowance from "Dad." I mean, I knew they were father and daughter, but there was just something about her calling him "Dad" that struck me. I suddenly realized that she was the only person in the world who could address him as Dad. He was Mr. President to the rest of us! The second was the access she had to him. Very important people wait months and possibly years to get an audience with the president if they ever get to see him at all. But she was able to scamper in and see him without notice.

In Romans 8:15, Paul uses the word *abba* to describe our relationship with God. *Abba* is an Aramaic word that means father, but it was only used for an intimate relationship between a child and his father. It would be like a child calling his father "daddy" in today's vernacular. The term is used only three times in the Bible—once by Jesus (Mark 14:36) and twice by Paul (Romans 8:15 and Galatians 4:6). Jesus used the term as He was appealing to His Father in an intimate conversation in the Garden of Gethsemane. Paul used it in the context of us being adopted as God's children.

There is a misconception that we are all children of God, but that is not biblical. God created us in His image, and He loves His creation dearly. But until we accept Jesus and His sacrifice for our sins, our relationship with God is still Creator and creation. There is only one way to become a child of God, and it is through His son, Jesus Christ. John says, "He came to that which was his own, but his own did not receive him. Yet to all who did receive him, to those who believed in his name, he gave the right to become children of God— children born not of natural descent, nor of human decision or a husband's will, but born of God" (John 1:11–13).

Because of Jesus's work on the cross, we are now joint heirs with Him. Paul said, "Now if we are children, then we are heirs—heirs of God and co-heirs with Christ, if indeed we share in his sufferings in order that we may also share in his glory" (Romans 8:17). In other words, God has adopted us as His children, and we have full rights to receive His inheritance along with our co-heir Jesus. Our relationship with God is now a family relationship!

What a privilege to be able to call Him Abba, Father. Just as Chelsea was able to call President Clinton "Dad" and have access to him whenever she needed him, we can call our heavenly Father "Dad" and have an audience with Him any time. Like President Clinton, our Father is never too busy for his child!

Father, help us fully realize our privilege in being able to call You Abba, Father, and enjoy direct access to You. As the perfect Father, You always know precisely what is best for each of us. Thank You for not giving us everything we want but always supplying everything You know we need. Forgive us when we grumble as ungrateful children. Help us see that Your plan for each of us is perfect if we will only trust You. Amen.

Darkness Exposed

This is the verdict: Light has come into the world, but people loved darkness instead of light because their deeds were evil. Everyone who does evil hates the light, and will not come into the light for fear that their deeds will be exposed.

-John 3:19–20

AS A SECURITY professional, I understand the value of light. When I have to secure a facility, I don't address alarms, cameras, or physical security until the exterior is well-lit with no areas of darkness that can be used for concealment. I learned the dangers of darkness early; my parents always told me to be in the house when the streetlights came on. Later in life, as a Secret Service supervisor, I would always encourage the young agents to be in their rooms before midnight because "nothing good ever happens after midnight." Crime statistics back me up on this: you are much more likely to be a victim of crime after dark.

This is what John meant when he said, "Everyone who does evil hates the light, and will not come into the light for fear that their deeds will be exposed" (John 3:20). There is no doubt that darkness provides concealment for evil. But in recent years and with the advance of technology, darkness has started showing up in well-lit places, namely our homes.

In 2006 when I was the special agent in charge of the Chicago Field Office, we partnered with the National Center for Missing and Exploited Children (NC-MEC) to target online child predators operating anonymously on the internet. While parents thought their children were safe at home and in their rooms, predators were online having discussions with the kids and doing all kinds of sordid things right under the parents' noses.

We had one of our agents from the Electronic Crimes Squad go online as a 13-year-old girl to see what kind of activity would turn up. The results were astonishing! Within a couple days, men from all over the targeted northern Indiana area were clamoring for the attention of who they thought was a young girl. They would ask for photos or videos and send inappropriate pictures of themselves. This continued for several weeks until we had enough evidence to arrest many of them. We picked the 24 most egregious suspects and put together cases on them.

After choosing a day for the arrests, we set up locations and times for 11 of the suspects to meet the "13-year-old girl." I doubted whether more than one or two would show up at their appointed time, but we thought it was worth a try. To my absolute surprise, each of them showed up on schedule, and we arrested them one by one. The remaining 13 were indicted and arrested over the following weeks.

The backgrounds of the defendants were not what I expected at all. Very few had prior criminal records. Many were married and had children. Most had good jobs and careers, including business owners, a builder, and even girls' basketball coaches. Some were even active church members and leaders in their communities. The one thing most had in common was that they had started looking at internet porn, progressed to child pornography, and ended up actively searching for child victims from the privacy of their own homes. Few would have ended up in this position had they not had such easy and private access to depraved and dark sites on the internet. The sad thing was it was like shooting fish in a barrel! If we had the resources, we could have continued the operation and arrested many more, but we were hoping that once the news got out, it would have a chilling effect on these heinous crimes against our youth.

Today we are seeing more and more people, including pastors and church leaders, caught up in this dark part of the internet. You no longer have to go out to insidious physical locations under the concealment of darkness for fear of being exposed. You need one private place in your house, and the darkness will come to you. You can even download software and access a site called the "dark web," where all of your evil acts will be kept anonymous.

John says that man in his natural state loves darkness because sinful man feels he can escape God and man's scrutiny by hiding in the shadows. Man has been doing this since Adam and Eve tried to hide from God in the garden of Eden. But God is light, and darkness will never overcome the light. John says, "The light shines in the darkness, and the darkness has not overcome it" (John 1:5). Darkness, after all, is not a thing but simply an absence of light. If you don't believe me, try introducing darkness into a well-lit room. It can't be done!

Throughout the Bible, light is contrasted with darkness. Light always represents righteousness and darkness evil. Those of us who follow Christ live in the light but often have dark private areas in our lives that we don't want anyone to know about. Often, it involves things we keep going back to on the internet.

Jesus said, "There is nothing concealed that will not be disclosed, or hidden that will not be made known. What you have said in the dark will be heard in the daylight, and what you have whispered in the ear in the inner rooms will be proclaimed from the roofs" (Luke 12:2–3). Jesus says that light will eventually expose all things done in the dark. Interestingly, He does not say when they will be disclosed but warns us with all certainty that they will be exposed. In the cases of the 24 men we arrested, their deeds done in the dark were revealed during this lifetime, resulting in ruined reputations, the loss of family trust, and years in prison. With others, their deeds may not come to light until the time of their deaths, when information comes out that tarnishes their legacy. Still, others may be able to take their dark secrets to their grave, but they will come to light and be exposed on the Day of Judgment. No one gets away with things done in the dark; Jesus said they would all be exposed.

For Christians, it is even more tragic when things they have done in the dark come to light because of the way it hurts the cause of Christ. We have seen pastor after pastor brought down by moral failures. It breaks my heart when I hear of these because I know the media and the world love to celebrate these failures. But even more damaging is the effect it has on young believers who have followed and been mentored by these pastors. It so often shakes them and causes them to question their own faith.

I have always made a point never to send an email or any electronic message that I wouldn't have a problem with everybody reading because I never know who might end up with access to it. In the same way, as followers of Christ, we must live knowing that everything we do, even in the dark, will one day be exposed and brought to light. When we finally accept this reality, we will stop frequenting dark places.

Father, help us to walk in Your light. Give us a keen awareness of Your constant presence and the dangers of thinking we can operate in the shadows out of Your sight. Holy Spirit, give us the strength to resist temptation, for it surrounds us every day, even in the most ordinary places. We pray these things in Your Son's name, Amen.

Invisible People

———— ✦ ————

Brothers and sisters, think of what you were when you were called.
Not many of you were wise by human standards; not many were
influential; not many were of noble birth.
-1 Corinthians 1:26

LESLIE WAS NOT the kind of fifth-grader you would seek out as a friend. He was an average-sized kid with disheveled curly blond hair that was never combed, his secondhand clothes never fit right, and he was always a little bit weird. These traits made him a favorite target for the other fifth graders to bully on the playground. Leslie always took it and seemed almost grateful that he was at least getting a little attention.

I was new at the Belmead, Texas, elementary school, and my family had just arrived from the foreign mission field in the Caribbean for a one-year furlough. I was somewhat reserved but made friends relatively quickly and had been accepted pretty well as a new student. I had noticed the other kids picking on Leslie, and while I didn't participate, I never did anything to try to stop it.

One day, as my younger sister and I were walking home from school, I noticed a group of kids gathered around what appeared to be two boys fighting. As we got closer, I saw that one of the ringleaders in my class had pinned Leslie to the ground and was dripping large globs of spit onto Leslie's face while all the other kids were laughing and egging him on. A wave of anger overcame me, and I dropped my books, pushed through the group, grabbed the kid by the collar, and dragged him off Leslie. He continued to hold on to Leslie's shirt with one hand, so I dug my heel into his arm until he finally let go. The onlookers looked stunned as I helped Leslie to his feet and pushed him down the sidewalk away from the group. It didn't take long for the mob to recover, and they started following us down the street hurling insults and threats.

When I got home, I went to my room and lay on the bed. I knew what I had done was right, but that didn't make me feel better. Like every other kid, I wanted to be liked and accepted by my peers, but I had blown it. I was overwhelmed with dread at the thought of returning to school the next day.

The following morning, I feigned every sickness I could think of, but my mother saw through it and pushed me out the door to go to school. As I walked into my classroom, I felt like a stranger—like the first day in a new school all over again. To make matters worse, when we went out to recess, Leslie followed me around like a puppy, excited about his new best friend. It was a lonely and awkward feeling. I sat on the ground against the chain-link fence and watched as several popular kids chose sides to play football. As is always the case, several didn't get chosen by either team and wandered off alone to watch. I realized I had never even noticed those kids before! I was fast, reasonably athletic, and big for my age, so I had always been chosen by one team or the other, never paying any attention to those sitting on the sidelines.

One such boy was Early B. Texas was still in the initial days of school integration, and Early B. was the only African-American kid in the fifth grade. Not wanting to listen to any more of Leslie's incessant chattering, I got up, wandered over, and sat next to Early B. We sat in silence for a while, and then a couple of the other football game rejects came and sat next to us. Again, there wasn't much conversation, but at least we didn't have to sit out by ourselves.

Over the following weeks, Early B. and I became friends, and I got to see the world from a different perspective. It was a world in which we would go off and do our own thing, completely separate and unnoticed by everyone else. I realized the established kids would never accept me because I had challenged the status quo. I was relegated to the invisible group that came and went unnoticed. I was only at the school for one year, and my family moved back to the mission field. But during that short year, I got a little taste of what it was like to be on the outside looking in.

Jesus dealt mainly with invisible people, people whom no one would have ever chosen to do anything of significance. At the time of Jesus, basic education for boys started at five or six and went until they were twelve or thirteen. Secondary education after that was reserved for the gifted or those considered to have potential, and they had to be chosen by the local rabbi. All others were dismissed to learn a trade and livelihood. Interestingly, not one of Jesus's disciples was from this pool of gifted men. Then He ministered to the blind, diseased, crippled, and socially unacceptable—all invisible and nameless people whom the world passed by every day.

Had I put together the plan for the Messiah to come, I would have had Him born in Jerusalem to an influential family. He would have had the best schooling, and His twelve followers would have been the brightest and the best. He would have performed flashy miracles in Jerusalem, more visible to the rich and powerful. His means of transportation would have been an upgrade from the donkey He used on his triumphal entrance into Jerusalem. But my plan would have failed miserably!

Paul said, "Brothers and sisters, think of what you were when you were called. Not many of you were wise by human standards; not many were influential; not many were of noble birth. But God chose the foolish things of the world to shame the wise; God chose the weak things of the world to shame the strong. God chose the lowly things of this world and the despised things—and the things that are not—to nullify the things that are, so that no one may boast before him" (1 Corinthians 1:26–29).

According to Paul, the problem with my plan is that the gospel does not work for the self-sufficient who think they have it all together. The Pharisees, Sadducees, and religiously powerful came from that pool of promise and potential, yet they were so self-absorbed that they couldn't see the Messiah standing right in front of them. Paul said that God chose the lowly and despised because they would depend on Him for their salvation, not their abilities and strengths.

We all get excited when a celebrity or someone of influence joins the faith. Yet, there are so many invisible people we pass every day, some even walking the hallways of our churches, whom few notice or care about. These were the types of people Jesus focused on. He wasn't impressed by fame, wealth, or influence.

I remember hearing testimony by Pastor Jim Cymbala several years ago that heavily impacted me. He said that he had just finished his third sermon at the Brooklyn Tabernacle on an Easter Sunday and was worn out. Many people had come forward to accept Christ, but as he was standing and facing the congregation, he saw a disheveled man with matted hair and missing teeth standing in the aisle about five rows back, looking at him. Pastor Cymbala said that he could tell the man wanted to come forward and talk to him and his first thought was, "What a bummer. I'm going to have to give him money." The pastor waved the man forward, and as he got within a few feet of him, he smelled the most awful odor: a mix of urine, sweat, and alcohol. He asked the man his name and found out it was David. David had been lying on the sidewalk outside the building next to the church, heard the music, and came in. Pastor Cymbala asked where he was living, and David said he had been staying in an abandoned truck because the homeless shelters had gotten too dangerous. Pastor Cymbala reached into his back pocket, took out his wallet, and tried to give David a $5 bill. David pushed the money away and said, "I don't want your money. I want this Jesus you were talking about." At that moment, Pastor Cymbala forgot all about David and realized how unloving he had become. The Lord had sent someone searching for Jesus, and he had tried to give him a couple of dollars to make him go away. He asked God for forgiveness, and God answered with a great flood of love. He embraced David, and as they embraced, the Lord said, "You know that smell? If you can't love that smell, I can never use you because the whole world smells that way to me. All the stinking filthy sin of mankind—I sent my son to die for that smell."[11]

This should be an important lesson for all of us. We need to take the blinders off and start noticing the Leslies, Early B's, and Davids out there who, in the world's eyes, have never been chosen for anything and never considered to have any potential. These are the ones who had a special place in our Savior's heart because there was no pride or self-sufficiency; they were totally reliant on Him. We can learn a lot about the love of the Father by getting outside our comfort zones and seeing people as He sees them. The interaction will teach us a lot about ourselves and exhibit the genuineness of our faith.

Father, forgive us for our pride, arrogance, and prejudice. We are who we are only because of Your grace and mercy, not because of anything we have done to deserve it. May we use our gratitude as motivation to reach out to others who are less fortunate. Open our eyes to the many needs around us and show us how we can serve others. Amen.

Honor the Emperor

Show proper respect to everyone, love the family of believers, fear God, honor the emperor.
-1 Peter 2:17

MY WIFE, JAN, taught fourth grade at a Christian school in Virginia while I was on the Presidential Detail in the mid-1990s. Most of her students came from conservative Christian families who wanted to ensure their children received an education with a Christian worldview. A disturbing trait she quickly noticed was that whenever she mentioned President Clinton's name in class, the children would boo and hiss. Jan would gently chastise them and remind them that we should honor the office of the presidency, even if we do not always agree with the person who occupies the office. More concerning still was that she knew her students were parroting what they heard at home.

As a conservative Christian myself, I got a unique view of what conservative Christians looked like from the Clintons' point of view, and it wasn't pretty. While I did not agree with many of President Clinton's policies, I was embarrassed by the total disrespect and disdain that so-called Christians held for the president. Because of this attitude, I could clearly see conservative Christians having less and less influence over the president and his decisions because they were critical no matter what he did.

The book of 1 Peter was written in approximately 64–67 AD. Nero was the emperor at that time, and his persecution of Christians was escalating in the Roman Empire. Rome burned in 64 AD, and by historical accounts, Nero blamed the fire on the Christian community, adding to the disdain many people had for Christians. If anybody had a reason to despise the emperor, it was Peter, but it was in this context that he wrote, "Submit yourselves for the Lord's sake to every human authority: whether to the emperor, as the supreme authority, or to governors, who are sent by him to punish those who do wrong and to commend those who do right" (1Peter 2:13–14). He goes on to say, "Show proper respect to everyone, love the family of believers, fear God, honor the emperor" (1 Peter 2:17). Peter said that we are to submit to and honor the emperor "for the Lord's sake." In other words, we should be the best citizens possible simply because we represent the Lord.

This doesn't mean that we blindly follow without being politically involved or letting our voices be heard. But it does mean that once our nation's leaders make decisions, we must do our best to submit to those decisions if they do not directly contradict God's Word. Each one of us must decide what that looks like in our own lives, but it must be done with good conscience without malice and hatred for our government leaders. Paul says, "Therefore, it is necessary to submit to the authorities, not only because of possible punishment but also as a matter of conscience" (Romans 13:5).

Our nation is currently so politically divided that we have difficulty separating our strong political beliefs from our spiritual beliefs and commitment to Jesus's teachings. If our side is not in power, we are automatically against every decision made. When we do this, we lose any influence we might have had, and the division and hatred grow.

So how do we overcome the negative feelings that have become deeply rooted sins in our lives? Jesus himself said, "But I tell you, love your enemies and pray for those who persecute you" (Matthew 5:44). What does praying for our enemies do? For one thing, it softens our hearts towards them.

An Al-Qaeda training manual distributed to Al-Qaeda operatives in the early 2000's instructed them always to put a hood over their hostages' heads when they took them captive. As long as the hostage-takers could not see the captive's face and eyes, they didn't think of the hostage as a person. When we conducted Hostage Survival Training for Samaritan's Purse employees working in high-risk environments overseas, we stressed the importance of the hostage to get their faces uncovered through whatever means necessary. They may have to persist for days, pushing the envelope to get the hostage-takers to let them raise their hoods a little bit at a time. At first, they may be able to uncover their mouth and nose, but the goal was to finally uncover the eyes. At that point, that hostage becomes a person to the hostage-taker, and the hostage can start taking steps to personalize themselves with their captors by talking about things they and their captors have in common. This personalization process makes it much more difficult for the hostage-takers to harm or kill the hostage if things turn deadly.

We think of our elected leaders just as hostage-takers think of their captives. They are hooded objects and targets of ridicule. Sincere and personal prayer for our leaders begins to lift that hood. As the hood starts to come up, we begin to personalize them and think of them as fellow human beings created by God. Sure, they have different political views, but is that justification for hate that only destroys us spiritually?

As a side note, if you are going to pray for our nation's leaders sincerely, you must turn off the politically divisive news shows and commentaries that elicit strong emotions and make millions out of sowing discord. Praying for our leaders while watching these news shows is like being an alcoholic who is desperately trying to stop drinking yet insists on walking through a bar every day. It won't work! As Paul says, "Finally, brothers and sisters, whatever is true, whatever is noble, whatever is right, whatever is pure, whatever is lovely, whatever is admirable – if anything is excellent or praiseworthy- think about such things" (Philippians 4:8). It is with this attitude that we are to pray for our leaders.

Lord, we pray for our attitudes toward our nation's leaders. We have become so divided in our country that we have confused our responsibilities as followers of Christ with political activism, resulting in bitterness and hatred toward opposing political views. Lord, this is not of You and destroys our Christian witness. Help us speak the truth calmly and in love, and give us the wisdom to know when to speak out and when to remain silent. Amen.

Make Your Days Count

A person's days are determined; you have decreed the number of his months and have set limits he cannot exceed.

-Job 14:5

DR. BILLY GRAHAM was a legend to me as I was growing up. My family sat together and watched his televised crusades and appearances on *The Tonight Show with Johnny Carson.* As a youngster, I went to Ridgecrest Baptist Encampment in Black Mountain, North Carolina, and hiked to the top of the mountain, where our guide pointed out the approximate location of Billy Graham's house across the valley. Never in my wildest dreams did I ever think I would one day work for his organization, but that was what the Lord had for me after I retired from the Secret Service.

Dr. Graham had retired and given up most of his public appearances by the time his son, Franklin, hired me to head up security for the Billy Graham Evangelistic Association and Samaritan's Purse. I had only a few personal interactions with Dr. Graham, yet each was memorable. As he neared the end of his life, I was asked to help plan his funeral and memorial service. There was no doubt it would be a big deal because of his influence on millions and his relationship with presidents, world leaders, members of Congress, and other influential people over the years.

My job was to oversee logistics and the security plans for the funeral motorcade from Asheville to Charlotte and the private funeral service for three thousand funeral guests, including the president, vice-president, and former presidents, in a large open tent in the parking lot of the Billy Graham Library in Charlotte. As I pulled together the Secret Service, FBI, North Carolina State Police, Charlotte

Police, and the sheriff's office for planning meetings, I was amazed at the cooperation and assistance from every level of law enforcement. It was a tribute to the impact Billy Graham had made on so many in the law enforcement community. Eventually, all plans were in place, from the timing of the motorcades to the transportation of guests through the maze of security that would be necessary because of the presence of the president and vice president.

On February 21, 2018, Dr. Billy Graham passed away quietly at his Montreat, North Carolina, home. Three days later, his funeral motorcade departed Asheville for the 100-mile trip to the Billy Graham Library in Charlotte, where the funeral service and burial would take place. The route and times were announced in the media, and thousands of people came to pay their respects to this man God had used in such an amazing way. The motorcade traveled through small towns and areas in Charlotte that had significance during Dr. Graham's life before its private arrival at the library. I stood on the sidewalk and watched as the procession stopped with all the police vehicles, shiny black funeral limousines, black Suburbans, and the long black hearse. Once everyone was in place, the back door to the hearse was opened, and the pallbearers and funeral directors removed the casket. I was struck by the contrast between the coffin and the pomp and circumstance surrounding the event. It was a simple, pine plywood casket with a plain wooden cross attached to the top. As I watched the procession slowly move into the library, I remembered the story Franklin shared with me regarding the casket several years before.

Over the years, the Grahams had formed a relationship with Warden Burl Cain at the notorious Angola State Prison in Louisiana, where the worst of hardened criminals were sent to do their time. Most inmates were serving life sentences or waiting on death row. Through this relationship with the warden, the Grahams had donated money for the building of two chapels at Angola and had held several evangelistic events at the prison for the inmates. At one of these events in 2005, Warden Cain showed Franklin the small woodworking shop on the prison grounds where caskets were made for the prisoners who passed away while incarcerated. Warden Cain explained that when he first arrived at Angola, the prison used state-issued caskets that were little more than heavy cardboard to bury deceased prisoners. One damp day as they were conducting a funeral for one of the inmates, the bottom of the coffin tore, and the corpse fell to the ground. Warden Cain knew that these men deserved better than that. They had paid their debt to society and merited a proper burial. He instructed the woodworking shop at the prison, staffed by inmates, to start making pine plywood caskets lined with comforters from Walmart for those who died while incarcerated at Angola. Franklin loved the simplicity and craftsmanship of the pine caskets with the cross on top and asked the warden if the prisoners might be able to make two for his parents. He further requested that each of the prisoners who worked on the caskets carve or burn their names on the foot of each coffin.

Late that night, as I was wandering through the empty library, making sure everything was in order for the public viewing the next day, I stopped and gazed at the casket. Here lay a man who had preached to over 200 million people, had been on the top-10 list of most admired men a record 61 times (the second closest was President Reagan at 31), who could pick up the phone and talk to any world leader at any time, resting in a simple pine coffin. I went to the foot of the casket and bent over where I could see the inscription, "Handcrafted by Richard Liggett, Paul Krolowitz, and Clifford Bowman." Liggett and Bowman had served life sentences for murder, and Krolowitz was incarcerated for armed robbery. While there wasn't much in common between the great man in the casket and the three criminals who had crafted it, all faced the same certainty—death. In fact, Liggett and Bowman both preceded Dr. Graham in death, dying in prison just a few years after completing the casket.

Most of us have intellectually accepted that death is a certainty but quickly put it out of our minds. Job said, "A person's days are determined; you have decreed the number of his months and have set limits he cannot exceed" (Job 14:5). The Bible declares that God has numbered our days from the time we are born, and we won't exceed that time by one minute, no matter what we do. I heard someone say that while we are counting up to determine how many days we have spent on earth, God started counting down our days at the time of our birth. There is much wisdom in thinking this way because instead of subconsciously counting up to infinity, we realize that every day we live is closer to zero. Dr. Graham realized death's inevitability, and many of his sermons reminded people of so. At former President Nixon's funeral, he famously reminded the family and guests that every one of them would eventually die. Another time, he said that one of the primary goals in life should be to prepare for death. Everything else should be secondary.

So why is it so important that we accept our mortality? Because our priorities will quickly change. In a commencement address at Stanford University toward the end of his life, Steve Jobs said, "Remembering that I'll be dead soon is the most important tool I've ever encountered to help me make the big choices in life. Because almost everything—all external expectations, all pride, all fear of embarrassment or failure—these things just fall away in the face of death, leaving only what is truly important."[12] While I don't know whether he had a relationship with Jesus Christ, Steve Jobs' statement was absolutely true. When we live as though we are dying, we mentally shift what's important. Our relationship with Jesus Christ becomes more meaningful, our love for family and others increases, and the materialism, distractions, and worries of this world decrease.

As I looked at the casket that night in the Billy Graham Library, I thought of Moses's words: "A thousand years in your sight are like a day that has just gone by, or like a watch in the night. Yet you sweep people away in the sleep of death— they are like the new grass of the morning: In the morning it springs up new, but by evening it is dry and withered" (Psalm 90:4–6). Though he lived 99 years, Dr. Graham understood the brevity of life. His eyes were on eternity, and his life was driven by his desire to share the gospel with as many people as he could while he was physically able. All indications were that at least two of the names on that casket, Richard Liggett and Clifford Bowman, became followers of Christ before their deaths, heavily influenced by the preaching of Billy Graham. The humble casket bearing their names confirmed that Dr. Graham placed more value on the souls of men than the things of this world. In Billy Graham's own words, "You cannot count your days, but you can make your days count."

Lord, thank You for the life and legacy of Billy Graham. Thousands of people will experience heaven due to his unashamed proclamation of the gospel for so many years. May we experience the same urgency he exemplified in knowing that our days are numbered, and may we make each one of them count for You. Amen.

I Can't Wear That Tie!

But whoever disowns me before others, I will disown before my
Father in heaven.
-Matthew 10:33

FATHER'S DAY AT our house always meant one thing: a new tie from at least one of the daughters. I would always play it up and act surprised, but I knew what was coming. My only anticipation was what kind of tie it would be because Jan always let them pick it out (and you never knew what a second or third-grader might consider fashionable).

One year, my youngest daughter, who was seven at the time, surprised me with a 101 Dalmatians tie. She proudly declared that it would go with all my suits! I couldn't argue with her because what color suit wouldn't go with a tie covered in black and white puppies? Her gleaming eyes showed she was delighted with the purchase and couldn't wait to see me wear it.

The following morning, I came downstairs wearing a shirt and tie, hoping that she had forgotten about her gift, but she immediately asked, "Aren't you going to wear your new tie today?" I dutifully went back upstairs to put on the 101 Dalmatians tie and secretly stuffed the tie I had taken off in my pants pocket. I went back downstairs, and her face again lit up when she saw me wearing her tie. While I ate breakfast, she sat there and named each of the puppies on my tie, identifying each one by the color of their collars. I finished breakfast, kissed the family goodbye, got in my car, and headed to work.

As I was driving to my assignment at the White House, I thought there was no way I could wear that tie into the office. The other agents at work were unmerciful, and wearing a tie like that would probably result in a new nickname. I had already outlasted nicknames such as "Big Mitts," "Big Foot," and "Chewbacca," so I didn't need to provide new ideas for additional names. As I pulled into the parking space at work, I quickly pulled my daughter's tie off and replaced it with the one I had stuffed in my pocket.

At the end of my shift at work, I went to my car, and there lying on the passenger seat was my daughter's tie. I hurriedly looked around to make sure nobody was watching, took off my tie, put her tie back on, and headed home.

She greeted me at the front door, and the first words out of her mouth were, "Did everyone like your new tie?" I felt like a jerk and the biggest hypocrite in the world! I had the chance to show everyone on the presidential detail how much I adored my daughter, even to the point of taking all the abuse and ribbing, and I had thought more about my reputation and image than showing my love for my daughter.

Isn't that how we treat Jesus? If we are around religious people with no threat of ridicule, we are happy to "put on our tie" and talk about Jesus and our faith. But put us into a situation where talking about Jesus could possibly get us derision or mockery, we "take off our tie" and hide it in our pocket.

Jesus issued a severe warning when He said, "But whoever disowns me before others, I will disown before my Father in heaven" (Matthew 10:33). He was forewarning His followers that they would be persecuted for the gospel. Early Christian teaching says all of them, except for Judas Iscariot and John, were eventually put to death for their faith. They never backed down and certainly never let the risk of mockery or jeering stop them.

So does Matthew 10:33 mean that denying Jesus at random times in our lives when we are under pressure would cause Jesus to deny us before His Father? Absolutely not! If that was the case, Peter's three denials at Jesus's trial under intense pressure would have disqualified him. Jesus was disappointed in him but quickly redeemed him. Besides, Paul says, "For it is by grace you have been saved, through faith—and this is not from yourselves, it is the gift of God—not by works, so that no one can boast" (Ephesians 2:8–9). Salvation is not earned by what we say or what we do. However, a life that is lived constantly denying Christ before men, either in word or deed, to accommodate reputations, business dealings, and social status clearly indicates that a person needs to examine themselves and their true belief in Jesus as Savior.

Just as I was regretful for not expressing love for my daughter when I had the opportunity, we should all feel ashamed when we neglect a chance to say something for Christ when the occasion presents itself. Peter certainly felt remorse. The Bible says that after his denials, Peter went out and wept bitterly. This is a sure sign of a repentant heart, and it should be the reaction we have when we fail our Lord. Like Peter, we should learn from our failures and strive to do better the next time an opportunity arises. Yes, this cowering disciple was the same Peter who several months later stood up on the Day of Pentecost before thousands and boldly proclaimed his allegiance to Christ.

By the way, I was able to redeem myself. A short time later, I wore the tie to the office, and sure enough, there was plenty of ribbing. But at the end of the day, everyone in the office knew how much I loved my daughter.

———————————————

Lord, give us the courage to take a stand for You. Most of us do not face physical persecution, but our pride and fear of damaging our reputations make us cowards. We face many opportunities every day to speak up for You, but most of the time, we remain silent. You gave up Your status and position as the creator of the universe, humbled Yourself to become a man, and died a shameful death for our sins. The very least we can do is acknowledge and honor You before men. Amen.

———————————————

For His Glory

<hr>

And there were many in Israel with leprosy in the time of Elisha the prophet, yet not one of them was cleansed—only Naaman the Syrian.
-Luke 4:27

ONE OF OUR *doctors has tested positive for Ebola.* These were the words I had feared ever since Samaritan's Purse and SIM Medical Missions had agreed to set up an Ebola treatment center at Elwa Hospital in Monrovia, Liberia. It was early 2014, and cases of the world's deadliest virus had popped up sporadically in the rural areas of Liberia and then crept closer and closer to Monrovia, where we had 20 or 25 employees.

As soon as the virus appeared in Liberia, we discussed the organization's risk tolerance for this dangerous disease and the conditions or redlines that would trigger an evacuation of our personnel. Without these triggers, an organization can quickly find itself drifting into a dangerous crisis without realizing it, much like a frog will remain in a slowly heating kettle of water unaware of the rising temperature. These triggers specified that employees' children and spouses would be evacuated when a certain number of Ebola cases were identified in Monrovia. When another level was reached, there would be another wave of employee evacuations. However, when the organization decided that Elwa would be an Ebola treatment center, these triggers went out the window, and we turned our attention to supporting our employees in the best way possible in their fight against this horrifying virus.

As part of our contingency planning, we contacted two of the best hospitals in Liberia to see if they could adequately treat any of our employees if they contracted the virus. It quickly became apparent that they were ill-equipped to handle Ebola patients at that time. Finally, we reached out to Doctors Without Borders (MSF), which had the most experience of any organization treating Ebola. They said their hospital in Brussels was the best-equipped hospital for handling Ebola patients, even though they had never had an active case. However, they were willing to accept our employees if they contracted the virus. It was settled; we would use our medical evacuation service to airlift any employee who contracted the Ebola virus to Brussels, where they could get the best possible treatment. In our minds, this part of the plan was in place, and we moved on to focus on other security-related issues in our contingency plan.

Two of our employees engaged in the fight against this deadly virus were Kent and Amber Brantly. I first met Kent and Amber in 2013 at Samaritan's Purse when they came through our required security training for new employees. Kent was a doctor, and he and Amber were on their way to their new assignment at Elwa Hospital in Liberia with their two young children. I didn't get to know them personally then, but that would soon change. They had only been at Elwa a few months when Ebola invaded Liberia. When Samaritan's Purse decided to stay and actively treat Ebola patients at the hospital, even though I knew what his response would be, I had our Director of International Security call Kent to get his personal feelings on this decision. Sure enough, Kent replied that he was a doctor and that God had called him to help the sick, no matter the disease. I have learned through the years that God's calling will always trump security concerns. My job was to pray and keep them as safe in that environment as possible while planning for the worse.

Kent and the other doctors and nurses trained for the inevitability of receiving Ebola patients. It involved the arduous task of donning and doffing Personal Protective Equipment (PPE) in a carefully regimented way, setting up an isolation unit, and learning the decontamination process. Every move had to be carefully choreographed and precise because any shortcut or sloppiness could result in contamination from the deadly virus.

Ebola victims slowly started trickling in, with the first two arriving in the back of an ambulance. One had died, and the other died several days later. The long hours dressed in the hot PPE were exhausting, discouraging, and emotionally draining. Of the first 13 patients Kent treated, twelve died. A morgue had to be set up behind the small hospital for the mounting casualties, and government vehicles would come by daily to carry away the body bags.

On July 20, Amber and their two young children departed Liberia for the United States to attend a relative's wedding. Kent, who had been working long hours and needed a break, was due a two-week vacation and planned on joining them the following week. However, events were about to take place that would forever change his life.

On Wednesday, July 23, Kent woke up with a low-grade fever and was just not feeling right. He called Dr. Lance Plyler, the Samaritan's Purse Team Leader, to let him know that he was running a temperature and thought it best to isolate himself. Kent reasoned that he probably had malaria, which is very prevalent in Liberia. With his busy schedule, he surmised that he had forgotten to take his malaria medication for several days. Throughout the day, he took two malaria tests, both of which came back negative, but he wasn't concerned because there are numerous strains of malaria, and the tests were specific to only one strain.

That evening, Kent's temperature continued to rise, so Lance decided to have several medical personnel suit up in PPE and draw blood from Kent for an Ebola test. Kent knew it would take three days to get the test results back, so he was stuck in his house for at least that amount of time, still believing that he probably had malaria.

The preliminary results of the test came back the following day negative for Ebola. However, Kent knew that it often takes three days for the Ebola virus to show up in the blood test. The true results were the ones that would come back on Saturday. Meanwhile, Kent was still running a high temperature, and his condition continued to deteriorate.

Saturday evening rolled around, and a knocking on his window awakened Kent. It was Lance. As Kent cleared the cobwebs from his head and focused in the direction of the window, he heard Lance say, "Kent, we got your test results, and I'm sorry to say that you are positive for Ebola."

At Samaritan's Purse Headquarters in Boone, North Carolina, the news of Kent's test results shocked us and initiated a flurry of activity. The whole focus of the organization turned to save Kent's life. This required us to get Kent to Brussels, where he could receive a higher level of care.

When I arrived at Samaritan's Purse, one of my first objectives was to contract with one of the most extensive and well-equipped evacuation services for such an emergency. I picked up the phone and called our representative, explained the situation, and said we needed to get Kent to the MSF hospital in Brussels. He said that he would get right back to me. An hour passed, and I had not heard from them, so I called again. The representative said they were still discussing the matter and would call me back. Finally, several minutes later, he called and said they would not be able to evacuate Kent. They said Ebola was a "different animal" from what they had ever dealt with before, and they were not equipped to perform such an airlift operation. I was in total disbelief! In my line of work, I always prided myself in having redundancy built into my contingency plans, but in this case, I had no backup plan!

I was on the Overseas Security Advisory Committee (OSAC) at the U.S. State Department, so I spent the next day and a half going through my contacts and calling State Department officials and private sector chief security officers for some of the largest companies that operated around the world. All were sympathetic, but none could offer assistance or suggestions. Many had the same evacuation company we did. It quickly became apparent that we were operating in unchartered territory. This, coupled with the growing sentiment in the media and public that no Ebola patient should be brought to American soil, gave me a sense of complete helplessness and hopelessness.

The following day, we had a crisis management meeting in Ken Isaacs' office. Ken was the vice president of projects for Samaritan's Purse, and the ministry in Liberia fell under his direction. In addition to Kent, we had about 25 other Samaritan's Purse employees that we needed to start thinking about evacuating. The window for this was quickly closing as more countries refused to accept travelers coming out of Liberia. The panic over Ebola was spreading worldwide. Ken had many things going on, so as I was leaving the meeting, he handed me a phone number and said, "These guys said they might be able to help us out with Kent."

I called the number, which was for Phoenix Air Group, and was told that everyone was in a meeting and that they would give me a call back when they were available. After waiting for an hour, I called again and received the same response. Finally, they called about two hours later. I asked if I could get a direct number to call them back and then headed to Ken Isaac's office so that we could both hear the conversation. From Ken's office, we called the number, which was answered by one of the pilots for Phoenix Air. He told us that they had the nation's only aircraft outfitted to transport someone with a highly contagious disease. He described it as a plastic bubble compartment inside a Gulfstream III. We eagerly asked if the aircraft could get Kent to the MSF hospital in Brussels. In a direct and no-nonsense tone, the pilot said, "You don't understand. No country in Africa or Europe will give us clearance to fly through their airspace with an Ebola patient. The only direction we can fly from Liberia is east toward the United States!"

Over the next few hours, Ken started communicating with Dr. Walters, Director of Operational Medicine at the State Department, who was also communicating with the Atlanta-based CDC. The next day we found that Emory University Hospital in Atlanta had agreed to accept Kent as a patient if we could get him there.

Back in Liberia, right after Kent's positive test for Ebola, Lance Plyler began researching other possible options for the treatment of Ebola. Through Dr. Lisa Hensley, a virologist from Maryland who had studied Ebola for several years, he learned about an experimental drug called ZMapp. It was a serum made of mouse antibodies grown on tobacco plants. The drug had shown promise but had never been administered to a human. There happened to be a course of the serum in Sierra Leone that was sent to a patient but never used. Lance arranged to have the unused experimental serum transported to Monrovia to be used as a last resort.

The Thursday after the positive Ebola test on Saturday, things had come together for Kent's evacuation to Emory Hospital, and the plane was in the process of heading to Liberia when we got word that Kent had taken a turn for the worse. His fever was high, and he was having trouble breathing. Lance, an experienced doctor, could tell Kent was fading fast. With that news, all work stopped at Samaritan's Purse Headquarters in Boone, and everyone started praying diligently for Kent. It was one of the most powerful prayer times I have ever experienced!

Lance had no other option and, with Kent's approval, decided to give him the experimental ZMapp. He had one of the medical staff administer the infusion through an IV while he watched through the window. As soon as the infusion started, Kent began to shake violently, and his breathing became extremely rapid. Lance called one of the doctors familiar with the experimental drug to describe what was taking place and was assured that this was good; the antibodies were fighting the virus! Within fifteen minutes of taking the ZMapp, Kent's temperature had dropped to 100, and his pulse had slowed considerably. Thirty minutes later, Kent was able to get out of bed and walk by himself to the bathroom.

The next day, the plane arrived in Monrovia, and Kent, in his full PPE, was transported to the airport for the long flight to Atlanta in his personal bubble. He was still very sick, but not at the point of death as he was the day before.

With Kent safely on board the evacuation flight, I turned my attention toward his arrival and taking care of his family in Atlanta. The subject of bringing someone with Ebola into the United States had become extremely contentious, and arrangements had to be made to ensure the family was not harassed by the media or the public. Franklin Graham had arranged to fly Amber, Kent's sister, and Kent's parents into Atlanta by private plane. I picked them up at the airport and took them to their hotel, where I had already checked them in under assumed names. As expected, Amber was anxious to get to Emory so she could be there when Kent arrived, but I told her it would be best if we waited to go to the hospital until Kent was settled into the unit. His impending arrival had received national attention, and I knew the situation at the hospital was going to be crazy.

Kent's flight was still several hours out, so I drove to Emory Hospital to see what the scene looked like. When I got there, I was stunned! Over thirty satellite and news trucks surrounded the building, with reporters all over the lawn and entrances to the hospital. I walked to the back of the hospital where Kent would be arriving and saw that the hospital police had the street blocked off, not allowing any pedestrian traffic. The plan was that if Kent were not mobile, they would bring him to the entrance on this back street and wheel his stretcher in through the rear entrance. If he were ambulatory, they would take him to an alleyway just outside the isolation unit where he would enter through a small back door.

When I returned to the hotel, Amber and Kent's family were glued to the television. All networks had cut away from their regular programming and were showing Kent's plane on the final approach. The plane landed in a secure area out of sight from the media, but a short while later, a motorcade of police cars surrounding two ambulances emerged through the airport gate heading toward Emory Hospital. The entire motorcade route was televised by media helicopters overhead. To my great relief, as the ambulance arrived at the hospital, it pulled to the alleyway outside of the Isolation unit, indicating Kent was strong enough to walk. The whole world watched as Kent, dressed in his bright white PPE, took those few steps from the back of the ambulance to the small back door of the hospital.

Amber and the family were elated, and I couldn't keep her at the hotel any longer. We jumped in the Suburban and headed to Emory, parking several blocks down the street from the hospital at a children's clinic to avoid crowds and media attention. We took the elevator to the basement and walked through a series of tunnels that took us under the streets and hospital, ascending a set of stairs just a few feet from the isolation unit. After a few minutes in the waiting room, the staff came and ushered Amber back to see Kent through the window in his unit. I must admit that I (or "The Gorilla," as the hospital staff referred to me) got teary-eyed. Kent was not out of the woods yet, but at least he was back with his family and not isolated in a small house alone on the other side of the world.

My wife and I stayed with Amber and her family as they came and went over the next few weeks. Kent improved every day and was finally released from Emory on August 21. After his release, I transported Kent and Amber to the mountains of North Carolina, where they stayed in a cabin for a few weeks to let the attention die down and allow Kent to continue recovering. I eventually accompanied them to Washington, D.C., where Kent and Amber met with President Obama and the secretary of Health and Human Services, and testified before Congress regarding the Ebola epidemic.

In November, I asked Kent and Lance Plyer if they would be willing to speak at the annual Overseas Security Advisory Committee (OSAC) meeting at the State Department. At the meeting were 2,000 of the nation's most influential government agency and private industry security officials. Kent and Lance told their stories and, without shame, gave God the glory for saving Kent.

In Kent and Amber's book, *Called for Life* (which I highly recommend), Kent wrestles with the tough question of why God chose to heal him while he allowed thousands of others to die from the terrible virus. This is a difficult question that many people ask when faced with cancer and other terminal illnesses.

The story of Naaman in 2 Kings 5 details how he was healed from the dreaded disease of that day—leprosy. Naaman was the military commander for one of Israel's most bitter enemies, Aram (present-day Syria). The King of Aram at that time was probably Ben Hadad II, who had gone to war several times against Israel under King Ahab. After those wars, Aram continued to send raiding parties into Israel, possibly led by Naaman, who would take captives back to Aram as slaves. It was through one of these little slave girls that Naaman heard of the prophet Elisha who would be able to heal him of his leprosy.

Jesus referred to the story as he was passing through Nazareth. He said, "And there were many in Israel with leprosy in the time of Elisha the prophet, yet not one of them was cleansed—only Naaman the Syrian" (Luke 4:27). This angered the crowd so much that they tried to kill Jesus. How dare He imply that God's healing was available to anyone but God's chosen people! Yet we feel the same way. When a follower of Christ gets cancer, we plead for God's mercy in their life and point out their faith and their close walk with Christ as a reason they should be healed. When it doesn't happen, we wonder why God would not take care of His own. But we must remember, as compassionate as Jesus was, He did not heal everyone. He healed only the one lame man at the pool of Bethesda in John 5. John says many others were there. Why did Jesus choose to heal this one and not the rest?

As I read through the miracles Jesus performed, I see three purposes for His healings: to show He was the Messiah from God as prophesied in the Old Testament, to show compassion, and to glorify His Father. The first purpose of healing continued through Jesus's lifetime and after through the work of the apostles. But we no longer live in the apostolic days, so that leaves us with the latter two reasons for God's intervention and healing today: his compassion and glory.

In the first several thousand years of God's dealing with His people, we see only a handful of physical healings. King Hezekiah was terminally ill and begged for God's mercy. God had compassion on him and gave him 15 more years. Another was Naaman, who was an enemy of Israel. So why did God choose to do it? I am not God, but I truly believe He did it for His glory. After he was healed, Naaman said, "Now I know that there is no God in all the world except in Israel" (2 Kings 5:15). The second most powerful man in the evil nation of Syria went home glorifying the God of Israel!

I still marvel at all the things that came together to save Kent's life, not the least of which was the single course of an experimental drug never used on humans, manufactured in Kentucky and sitting unused in Sierra Leone, and not overly effective in treating Ebola since. I am not God, and His ways are far beyond me. But in hindsight, and as I have seen God use Kent and Amber in the White House, Congress, media interviews, and their book, I do not doubt that, like Naaman, God saved Kent's life for His glory.

Lord, we know You are a compassionate Father with our best interest at heart. Thank You for Your healing touch and the assurance that You will never leave nor forsake us, no matter what we go through. Help us to look at our lives through the lens of eternity, fully realizing that physically, we all live in a terminal state, but knowing You will always provide healing for us, if not now, then in eternity. Amen.

An Unheeded Warning

He answered, "Then I beg you, father, send Lazarus to my family, for I have five brothers. Let him warn them, so that they will not also come to this place of torment."
-Luke 16:27–28

I RECEIVED A call one day in the Secret Service Memphis Field Office from a couple concerned brothers. They told me that their elderly father was caught up in a scam and had sent thousands of dollars overseas to a group of individuals promising to eventually share millions of dollars with him. This scam was known as advanced fee fraud, in which fraudsters contacted victims claiming they have millions of dollars tied up in a foreign country. They promised to share the millions with victims if they sent money upfront to help pay legal fees, bribes, and court costs to get the millions released.

It was hard to imagine that anyone would fall for this scam, but we received numerous reports of people who did. There were even instances of some who got so deeply involved that after first sending thousands overseas, they made trips abroad to "close the deal." It was an amazing psychological phenomenon that once a victim sent even a tiny amount of money to the fraudsters, they were hooked. The more money they sent, the more they believed they would get millions, no matter how often friends and family warned them.

This was the case with the two brothers in Memphis, who said that despite repeatedly warning their father that it was a scam, he sent more money and believed that he would reap a windfall in the end. They said that he was close to draining his life savings. The brothers asked if I would go out and speak with their father. Since I was a "subject matter expert," he would certainly listen to me.

143

I agreed, went to the father's address, and knocked on the front door. After identifying myself, I explained that his sons had asked me to come to talk with him. I told him that he was caught up in a scam, explained how it worked and gave examples of others who had lost their hard-earned money to these cons. I was shocked by his response! "Get off my property!" he yelled, "I don't need 'Big Brother' sticking his nose into my private affairs!"

In Luke, Jesus tells the parable of the rich man and Lazarus. Lazarus was a beggar who sat at the rich man's door, begging for any crumbs coming his way. Eventually, Lazarus and the rich man died. Lazarus went to a place of comfort by Abraham's side, while the rich man went to Hades, the place of torment. The rich man looked up, saw Lazarus next to Abraham, and said,

> 'Father Abraham, have pity on me and send Lazarus to dip the tip of his finger in water and cool my tongue, because I am in agony in this fire.'
> But Abraham replied, 'Son, remember that in your lifetime you received your good things, while Lazarus received bad things, but now he is comforted here and you are in agony. And besides all this, a great chasm has been set between us and you so that those who want to go from here to you cannot, nor can anyone cross over from there to us.'
> He answered, 'Then I beg you, father, send Lazarus to my family, for I have five brothers. Let him warn them, so that they will not also come to this place of torment.'
> Abraham replied, 'They have Moses and the Prophets; let them listen to them.'
> 'No, father Abraham,' he said, 'but if someone from the dead goes to them, they will repent.'
> He said to him, 'If they do not listen to Moses and the Prophets, they will not be convinced even if someone rises from the dead.' (Luke 16:24-31)

Jesus was saying that if men have hardened their hearts to the truth, not even someone coming from the dead, indeed a "subject matter expert," could persuade them.

Jesus's parable in Luke is a disturbing picture of hell. The rich man "longed for a drop of water to cool his tongue." Jesus referred to hell at least 70 times in the New Testament, yet preachers rarely preach on the subject anymore. If we believe that Jesus is who He said He was, then we must take His teachings on hell seriously.

Our attitudes toward hell today are flippant. Billy Joel wrote the song "Only the Good Die Young" in 1977. The lyrics for one of the verses state in essence that some people believe that there is a heaven for the saints, but he would rather go to hell with the sinners because they are much more fun. In his mind, hell is going to be a place to party and be with friends. These lyrics go against Jesus's teaching of hell as a place of torment and permanence. If hell were the party that Billy Joel sings of, the rich man would be looking forward to the day his five brothers could join him so they could be together. But hell was so terrible that the rich man wanted Lazarus to return and warn his brothers, even if he had to spend eternity separated from them. Abraham said that the prophets and the scriptures had warned them, and the warnings went unheeded. Someone coming back from the grave with personal knowledge of their impending doom would not make a difference.

We have downplayed the idea of hell to the point that it is no longer considered a bad destination. This, coupled with our misconceptions of heaven being a place where all we will do is stand in front of a bright spiritual being and sing for eternity, has made people like Billy Joel think hell would be their preference.

Like my warning to the elderly man in Memphis went unheeded, most people will ignore Jesus's multiple warnings of hell. They say that there is no way a truly loving God would ever send anyone to an eternal place of torment. Yes, he is a loving God and an incredibly patient God. But He is also a just God who cannot tolerate sin. He has done all He can by sending His Son to die, and providing a way of escape, but it is our choice now. Until we can truly comprehend eternity in a place absent of anything good, we will never appreciate the gift of salvation He has provided.

Lord, thank You for taking such extreme measures to provide a way for us to escape eternal judgment. That You were willing to come and endure such an excruciating death for our salvation should convince us of the terrible reality of an eternity in hell. Please forgive our lack of concern for the lost. We pray that You would rekindle the urgency in us to warn others who are on the path to destruction as we once were. Amen.

Training Our Minds

———◆———

Don't copy the behavior and customs of this world, but let God
transform you into a new person by changing the way you think.
Then you will learn to know God's will for you, which is good and
pleasing and perfect.
-Romans 12:2 (NLT)

IT HAS BEEN said that our life is like a tube of toothpaste. When we're squeezed, what's inside will come out. Paul and Silas were prime examples of this truth. When imprisoned and beaten, they sang and worshipped. Why? Because they had been transformed by the renewing of their minds. But what exactly does this entail?

Special Agent Tim McCarthy was one of my predecessors as the special agent in charge of the Chicago Field Office. You may remember Tim as the agent who was shot during the Reagan assassination attempt in 1981. Many of us consider Tim a hero because he turned toward the shooter as a human shield for President Reagan and took a round in the stomach. Tim would probably tell you differently. He would say that he acted instinctively based on hours and hours of training.

Newly hired Secret Service agents undergo a rigorous training program at the Secret Service Training Center in Beltsville, Maryland. They receive extensive instruction in firearms, self-defense, and driving, along with classroom training in multiple fields of investigation. One significant part of their training is the physical protection of the president, vice president, and their families.

An essential exercise in this training segment is the AOPs, or "Attack on Principal" exercises. These are staged scenarios with actors and trainers who replicate real-life situations in which the president may be involved. It may be a rope line, a parade, an arrival at a public event, or a campaign rally. The young trainees are assigned to protect someone playing the part of the president in the scenario. They never know if something is going to happen during the simulation, but if it does, they are responsible for responding appropriately. Sometimes someone in the crowd pulls a gun or a weapon. Occasionally someone is disruptive but not a threat, and other times nothing happens. These exercises heighten the senses of trainees, making them ready to react quickly if they see anything remotely unusual. If danger is detected, the agents are taught to do one of two things: immediately cover and evacuate the president or if the threat is within arm's reach, respond to it, even if it means lunging toward the barrel of a gun or knife. It has to be a split-second reaction without time to think. By the time they leave training, they have done so many exercises that their response is second nature and almost subconscious. This, however, is not the end of the training, as all agents continue AOP training throughout their careers to reinforce the developed instinct.

The brain is a remarkable thing! Psychologists will tell us that repetition is the most effective way of learning because it takes a learned behavior from the conscious to the subconscious, where it becomes instinctive. For instance, when we first learned to tie our shoes, it took a lot of brain energy and focus. After years of repetition, we don't even think about how to do it; it's just automatic. Our brains naturally seek efficiency, so when you do a task repeatedly, the skill gets moved to a different part of the brain where the subconscious takes over, and the action becomes automatic.

But there is a flip side. Repeated bad behavior also becomes automatic. Bad behavior must be strongly suppressed and new good behavior repeated and encouraged. Paul talks about this struggle when he says, "I do not understand what I do. For what I want to do I do not do, but what I hate I do" (Romans 7:15). Because of our sinful natures, we will always struggle with good and bad, but we must focus on repetitive training to develop the mind and character of Christ. This is called sanctification.

Paul said, "Finally, brothers, whatever is true, whatever is honorable, whatever is just, whatever is pure, whatever is lovely, whatever is commendable, if there is any excellence, if there is anything worthy of praise, think about these things" (Philippians 4:8). The reality is that whatever we put into our minds comes out as words and actions, just like the tube of toothpaste. If we continually ingest worldliness on television, the internet, and social media, that worldliness moves from our conscious and embeds itself in our subconscious where we don't even notice it anymore. On the other hand, if we are taking in and meditating on God's Word, reading and watching positive and uplifting material, our minds will be programmed with these thoughts.

But there is more to it than just thinking good thoughts. Paul says, "We demolish arguments and every pretension that sets itself up against the knowledge of God, and we take captive every thought to make it obedient to Christ" (2 Corinthians 10:5). He uses military terms to describe this war for the mind. It is a picture of a disciplined soldier who captures every evil thought and wrong desire before it can take root. It is essential to start every day in the Word and prayer. You will need this strength to resist, control, and take evil thoughts captive.

A positive and uplifting mindset is not natural to us—just as stepping in front of a bullet to save the president's life is not natural. It takes constant and repetitive training and resolve. But with the help of the Holy Spirit, we can move closer to what Paul calls the mind of Christ.

Lord, change us from the inside out. May our external actions be an outpouring of the transformation You have given us on the inside. I pray that Your Holy Spirit would guide our minds and thoughts so that the way we speak and act would be honorable, just, and pure, and represent You well. Amen.

The Haunting Portrait

I do not understand what I do. For what I want to do I do not do,
but what I hate I do.
-Romans 7:15

THE WHITE HOUSE can be a pretty creepy place at 2:00 in the morning. While the president and his family sleep upstairs in the residence, at midnight, the lights on the Ground Floor and the State Floor dim to a meager glow. You're left wandering the darkened floors, eerily watched by life-sized portraits of deceased former residents. At about 2:00 in the morning, those portraits start talking to you. By 4:00, you start answering them . . .

When I was working the midnight shift, I always enjoyed strolling through the historical mansion and reliving history. Down in the basement on the way to the bowling alley, I could look up and still see some of the char marks on the stone from when the White House was burned in the War of 1812. In the East Room, Abraham Lincoln, William McKinley, and John F. Kennedy, to list a few, had lain in repose after their deaths. On the wall is the large portrait of George Washington that Dolly Madison famously removed, rolled up, and took with her as she escaped the approaching British troops, who eventually burned the White House, in the War of 1812.

Most of the portraits in the White House were completed and approved by each president while he was still alive or by his family members if he died while in office. Each one tried to portray a grand image of self-confidence, strong leadership, and the look of a statesman who could handle any situation. This was the persona each one of them wanted to leave with us. In reality, these images were merely facades for some very flawed men. If you read through their modern-day

151

biographies, you quickly find that behind the scenes, many were alcoholics, womanizers, and egocentric, far from being the men of character and integrity portrayed in their portraits.

For me, the most intriguing presidential portrait in the White House was John F. Kennedy's, which was done posthumously, and I found myself staring at it repeatedly since it was right next to one of the posts we held on the State Floor. He is dressed in a drab brownish suit with his arms folded, his face downcast, and his eyes not visible. The story is that Jackie Kennedy did not want the same old photo of President Kennedy with the "bags under his eyes and his penetrating gaze." Mrs. Kennedy wanted him portrayed as a thinker and thus chose a picture of Ted Kennedy looking down at his brother's grave as a model for President Kennedy's portrait.

To me, the portrait depicted President Kennedy as a sad, somber, and lonely man with the weight of the world on his shoulders. I thought back to the failed Bay of Pigs invasion and the ensuing Cuban Missile Crisis when we were on the brink of a nuclear war with the Soviet Union for 13 days. I surmised that this was probably an accurate portrayal of President Kennedy during his short time in office. Had President Kennedy been alive when this portrait was completed, I am not sure he would have liked it or approved it, but to me, it was the most honest and genuine portrait in the White House.

Like those presidential portraits, every one of us wants to present a façade that says we have everything together. This has especially become prevalent in the age of technology. On their social media accounts, men and women present themselves as living the perfect lives with photos showing vacations, adventures, new possessions, and perfect kids. Others see these posts and become depressed because they are not experiencing the picture-perfect lives their friends are portraying. But I have a little secret for you: none of these families' lives are as perfect as they are trying to show. There is a good possibility there may be financial problems, marital difficulties, depression, anxiety, or many other flaws behind those ideal exteriors. There are no perfect lives.

To the public eye, the Kennedys had everything—wealth, influence, health, and good looks. In fact, the media dubbed their lives and surroundings as "Camelot" because of the appearance of perfection. But much has been written in recent years regarding President Kennedy's alleged moral failings and the serious psychological and physical issues he kept well hidden. In 2002, President Kennedy's medical records were released, showing a much different picture from the life the media had presented. The documents revealed that he took painkillers, anti-anxiety medication, stimulants, and sleeping pills. When the stress increased, he was taking eight medications a day. So much for the perfect life! The truth behind the facade is why I thought his portrait was the most genuine and honest portrait in the White House. It portrayed an ordinary man with struggles.

The Apostle Paul wrote at least 13 of the 27 books in the New Testament. He has been canonized, churches have been named after him, and his portrait is displayed in many stained-glass windows. Yet when he described himself, he said he was the "Chief of all sinners" (1 Timothy 1:15) and declared, "For what I want to do I do not do, but what I hate I do" (Romans 7:15). Paul was realistic and transparent about who he was. There was no facade of having it all together but an acknowledgment that he struggled with sin. We don't know what sins he might have wrestled with, but one was probably arrogance and conceit. He writes, "Therefore, in order to keep me from becoming conceited, I was given a thorn in my flesh, a messenger of Satan, to torment me" (2 Corinthians 12:7). He recognized this "thorn" as a way that God would make him humble and keep him grounded in reality.

Jesus had much to say about those who wanted to put on a front of perfection. In Luke 18, he tells the parable of the Pharisee and the tax collector:

> Two men went up to the temple to pray, one a Pharisee and the other a tax collector. The Pharisee stood by himself and prayed: 'God, I thank you that I am not like other people—robbers, evildoers, adulterers—or even like this tax collector. I fast twice a week and give a tenth of all I get.' But the tax collector stood at a distance. He would not even look up to heaven, but beat his breast and said, 'God, have mercy on me, a sinner.' I tell you that this man, rather than the other, went home justified before God. For all those who exalt themselves will be humbled, and those who humble themselves will be exalted. (Luke 18:10–14)

This is a sobering message to pretentious people who want to put on an air of perfection. You may dupe others for a while, but you will not fool God for a moment.

Perfection will not be attained in this lifetime, so if you see others living that "perfect life," you probably don't know them as well as you think. The sad thing is that these people are usually guarded in their relationships because they fear the exposure of their imperfections. Close relationships happen only when we embrace each other's imperfections, for only then do we see a genuine person. That is not to say that we shouldn't constantly strive to be more like Christ every day because he has set the standard. But just like Paul, we need to confess our imperfections and realize that we are a work in progress until we join Jesus in heaven.

I love the inscription on Ruth Graham's headstone. Ruth was the wife of Billy Graham, and the idea came from a road construction sign she saw as she was driving down a highway. Her headstone reads, "End of Construction—Thank you for your patience." These are not the words of a pretentious person. These are the words of a person who realizes their imperfection as they long for genuine perfection.

Father, we readily admit that we are imperfect people. Forgive our proud spirits that put on facades to make us look better than we really are. We realize that we will never achieve perfection here on earth, but may we never stop seeking and desiring to be more like you every day we live. Amen.

The Counterfeit Christian

"But he said, 'No, lest while you gather up the tares you also uproot the wheat with them. Let both grow together until the harvest, and at the time of harvest I will say to the reapers, "First gather together the tares and bind them in bundles to burn them, but gather the wheat into my barn."
-Matthew 13:29–30 (NKJV)

ON THE AFTERNOON of April 14, 1865, before he departed for Ford's Theater, President Lincoln ironically signed the bill creating the U.S. Secret Service. However, the Secret Service's original purpose was not to protect the president as it is today but to combat the rise of counterfeit currency after the Civil War. Then, one out of every three banknotes was counterfeit, causing significant harm to the economy. To this day, the Secret Service is the primary federal agency that investigates counterfeit currency.

All Secret Service agents go through counterfeit training in Secret Service school. The goal is not to make them experts in detecting counterfeit currency but to make them experts in how genuine money is printed. If you know all about the genuine article, you can quickly identify the counterfeit.

Numerous security features have been added to our currency in recent years to make it more difficult to counterfeit. However, there were three failsafe items I looked at to verify the authenticity of a bill—the security fibers, the paper, and the portrait.

The security fibers are tiny blue and red hairlike threads put into the paper when manufactured. These fibers become part of the paper, and on genuine currency, the tiny fibers can be lifted and moved around with a pin or a needle.

Counterfeit money either won't have these tiny fibers or will have them drawn on. Close examination of a counterfeit note will clearly show that the fibers are superficial and not actually part of the paper.

The paper for genuine currency is produced at Crane and Company Paper Manufacturing in Massachusetts and has been since 1879. The paper composition is 25 percent linen and 75 percent cotton, making it highly durable. It can take over 4,000 folds, forward and backward, before the bill will show any appreciable wear. Finding a paper that feels and looks like genuine paper is a considerable challenge to the counterfeiter. Seasoned bank tellers can quickly identify a counterfeit note just by the feel of the paper. I have seen tellers who can quickly flip through a two-inch stack of bills and promptly detect the counterfeits without even looking at them. The biggest problem with counterfeit paper is that it will not hold up. Once it has been in someone's pocket for a while or passed two or three times, it is already tearing and coming apart.

The portrait on genuine currency is printed by the intaglio method, meaning the ink is raised above the paper's surface. You can feel the raised ink if you run your fingernail over the portrait on a genuine bill. It gives the picture a lifelike, three-dimensional look, especially if you look in the eyes. The counterfeiter has a difficult time with the portrait because he is printing the money by offset press or desktop publishing. The portrait is printed flat on paper and looks one-dimensional and lifeless, especially the eyes.

So now that I have made you an expert in detecting counterfeit currency, let's apply these principles to counterfeit Christians or the tares in Jesus's parable found in Matthew 13. The story goes that the farmer planted a wheat seed, but during the night, his enemy came and sowed tares (weeds) in with the seed. The wheat and tares came up together and looked so much alike that the farmer told the workers to wait and just let them grow together, fearing that if they tried to pull up the tares, some of the wheat would also be uprooted. The wise farmer said that at the time of harvest, they would separate the wheat from the tares and burn them.

Over the years, as I have worked on counterfeit investigations; I have noticed many similarities between counterfeit notes and counterfeit Christians. Both try to imitate the genuine article as closely as possible, to fool as many people as possible. But there are certain traits and characteristics that the genuine note or Christian will have that the counterfeit will never be able to duplicate.

The security fibers represent God's Word that is woven into us as part of our lives. James says, "Do not merely listen to the word, and so deceive yourselves. Do what it says" (James 1:22). The parable of the Good Samaritan is a prime example. The priest and the Levite knew the Scriptures and probably had them memorized, yet it was all superficial and for show. They passed by the injured man because God's Word was not woven into their everyday lives like genuine fibers. Jesus said, "Not everyone who says to me, 'Lord, Lord,' will enter the kingdom of heaven, but only the one who does the will of my Father who is in heaven" (Matthew 7:21).

The genuine paper speaks of our perseverance. James says, "Consider it pure joy, my brothers and sisters, whenever you face trials of many kinds, because you know that the testing of your faith produces perseverance. Let perseverance finish its work so that you may be mature and complete, not lacking anything" (James 1:2–4). The way people handle adversity says a lot about the genuineness of their faith. Like the fragile paper of a counterfeit note, it doesn't take much hardship in a counterfeit Christian's life for them to come apart and turn their backs on God. As Charles Spurgeon famously said, "A Bible that's falling apart usually belongs to someone who isn't." A quick read through *Fox's Book of Martyrs* will show time and time again how through history genuine Christian lives never came apart, even under extreme hardship and persecution.

The term "Christian" was first used in Antioch and means "Little Christ." While it was meant as a derogatory term, it turned into the highest compliment someone could give a follower of Christ. I previously said that the portrait on a genuine bill looks three-dimensional and lifelike because the ink is raised above the surface of the paper. In contrast, the portrait on a counterfeit bill looks flat and lifeless. When people look at us, what do they see? Do they see a fuzzy image that might be the image of Christ, or do they see a clear, three-dimensional portrait that is striving to take on the likeness of Christ?

As counterfeit notes are seized across the country, they are inventoried and forwarded to Secret Service headquarters in Washington, D.C., where they are eventually destroyed. It is a sobering parallel to what will happen to the tares at harvest: "tied into bundles and burned."

It may be difficult for us to tell the difference between genuine and counterfeit Christians. But the Bible says that it is not our responsibility; that will be done at harvest time. Our job through introspection is to ensure that we are the wheat, not the tare.

———————————

Lord, I pray that You will give us a firm assurance of our salvation. But for those who are not sure whether they are the wheat or the tare, I pray that they would quickly get it settled with You. So many people, even in our churches, know what a Christian should look like and imitate it. But it's not what we look like on the outside; it's what's on the inside. Lord, we want to be the genuine article. Amen.

———————————

All Things to All People

---- ✦ ----

To the weak I became weak, that I might win the weak. I have
become all things to all people, that by all means I might save some.
-1 Corinthians 9:22

THE MOST CHALLENGING assignment I ever received as a Secret Service agent was to be the lead advance agent for First Lady Hillary Clinton for the Beijing Women's Conference in September 1995. The diplomatic relations between China and the U.S. were not good because of trade differences and human rights issues, and the last thing China wanted was 50,000 women activists converging on Beijing all at once. It had been only six years since the Tiananmen Square massacre of protesters, and the Chinese did not want another world spectacle in handling "angry women." Having the first lady there added pressure because of the increased global media attention it brought.

I felt the chilly reception as soon as my team and I stepped off the plane in Beijing. We were assigned two "taxis" by Chinese state security and were always required to use these vehicles as we moved around Beijing. Clearly, they wanted to know where we were and what we were doing at all times. We assumed these vehicles had listening devices planted in them, as was probably the case with our hotel rooms. Any private conversations we needed to have had to be conducted in a special room in the middle of the U.S. Embassy.

For the first several days, we surveyed the hospitals, looked at the different sites Mrs. Clinton would be visiting, and ran motorcade routes. In the afternoons, we would meet with the Chinese security hierarchy and make requests for assets or support. Unfortunately, they would try to negotiate with us or deny our requests.

My frustrations were quickly rising as the day of Mrs. Clinton's arrival rapidly approached, and we were far from having things nailed down.

The real problem came two days before Mrs. Clinton's arrival. The U.S. Air Force cargo jet (C-141) transporting Mrs. Clinton's limo and follow-up vehicle, along with fifteen additional Secret Service agents, was five hours from landing in Beijing. The head of the Chinese security unit we were working with came to me and said that he would be the one riding in the right front seat of our limo while Mrs. Clinton was in Beijing. I told him that we had a strict policy that the front seat was reserved for Mrs. Clinton's personal detail leader, but he would be welcome to ride in the follow-up vehicle right behind the limo. He looked me squarely in the eyes and said, "We have not yet cleared your air force cargo jet to land in Beijing." He certainly had me over a barrel! In desperation, I finally said, "Okay, you can share the front seat with Mrs. Clinton's detail leader." At first, he said that was not acceptable, but after some negotiations back and forth, he finally agreed to the arrangement, and the Air Force C-141 was allowed to land.

On the way back to the hotel, I was livid. I was going to have to call Washington, D.C., and tell the detail leader why he would have to share his front seat with a burly Chinese security agent. I wondered what other surprises I would endure over the next several days when my soft-spoken Chinese interpreter said, "You need to take the Chinese security men out, drink some rice wine, and have a nice dinner with them. Hosting someone for wine and dinner is a big deal in Chinese culture and is a sure sign of respect and friendship." Being raised a "tea-to-taler" and a Southern Baptist, that idea had not crossed my mind. I had no issue with other people drinking, and I couldn't find anything in the Bible that forbade drinking wine, but that just wasn't me or how I wanted to spend the evening. However, if it would give me a connection with these guys resulting in some co-operation, I decided I would try to embrace their cultural customs of friendship.

When we returned to the hotel, I contacted the director of Chinese security and invited him and his two assistants to the hotel for dinner that evening. They readily accepted, and we agreed to meet in the restaurant at 7:30. They arrived on time, and we were shown to the table I had reserved in the corner. The atmosphere was a little tense with the formalities, so when the waiter arrived, I asked my Chinese guests if they would like some wine before their dinner. They each ordered a glass of rice wine and then looked at me expectantly to see if I would join them in this drink of friendship. After a bit of hesitation, I had the waiter bring me one also. As the wine arrived, they began to loosen up and relax. They asked me if I had ever had rice wine before, and I told them I had not. One of them lifted their glass and offered a toast, and we all took our first sip. I have never tasted kerosene before, but I am sure it tastes much like rice wine. My guests must have seen the grimace on my face because they began to laugh. That was the ultimate icebreaker! After that and throughout the dinner that night, we told stories, talked about our careers, and laughed. It had nothing to do with the wine itself because I did not take another sip. It was all about the fact that I was willing to respect and experience their culture.

The next day was completely different from what I had experienced the previous five days. The Chinese security officials picked me up at the hotel, and we ran motorcade routes, reviewed arrival and departure areas, and discussed the schedule. They couldn't have been more cooperative! I invited them to have dinner with me again that night at the hotel restaurant to iron out any last-minute issues before Mrs. Clinton's arrival the following day.

Mrs. Clinton flew in the next day, and her two-day visit went flawlessly. We worked side by side with our Chinese counterparts, and a real comradery formed because of the mutual respect and understanding we had developed for each other.

Mrs. Clinton flew out on the third day, and as we watched her plane disappear over the horizon, the Chinese security director shook my hand and said he was hosting a dinner that night for my three advance team members and me. He wanted to celebrate Mrs. Clinton's successful visit and the excellent relationship between our agencies.

We arrived at the hotel ballroom that night to find 30 Chinese security officials attending the dinner. I was seated just to the right of their security director. As the dinner was getting ready to start, the head waiter brought a bottle of traditional wine, poured a little into my wine glass, and then stepped back and waited for my approval as the guest of honor. The room became quiet, and all eyes were on me. Refusing the expensive wine would have been a severe slap in the face to their culture, and all inroads I had made with them would have been lost. Fortunately, I had seen this done on television, so I picked up the glass, swirled it around, took a sip, and swished it in my mouth. From the corner of my eye, I could see my Secret Service team straining to control themselves because they knew I did not drink and had no clue what I was doing. I nodded my approval to the waiter, and he began pouring the wine into glasses all around the table. For all I knew, it could have been prune juice! After the wine had been poured, we all stood, and the security director toasted the friendship between our organizations.

This experience taught me a valuable lesson. Sometimes you must step out of your comfort zone and the safety of your traditional views before you can genuinely connect with someone from a different culture or background. Jesus did this repeatedly when He associated with the Samaritan woman, tax collectors, prostitutes, and criminals. He always approached them on their turf and in their world to make that connection before drawing them into His world.

Paul was also a master at this. He shared the gospel with the Jews from the perspective of a Jew talking about the law and God's covenants, eventually tying it to Jesus Christ, the expected Messiah. At the same time, he participated in Jewish traditions and cultures to avoid offending the Jews. He spoke of the God of Creation to the Gentiles who had many gods. As he was walking around Athens, he was distressed at all the idols. But instead of criticizing and "preaching" at them, he said, "Men of Athens, I notice that you are very religious in every way, for as I was walking along I saw your many shrines. And one of your altars had this inscription on it: 'To an Unknown God.' This God, whom you worship without knowing, is the one I'm telling you about" (Acts 17:23). Once again, he stepped into their culture and established that relationship before sharing the gospel. Was he compromising himself? Absolutely not! Paul understood that evangelism is relational; he had to find common ground with someone before sharing the gospel. If you don't do this, you are just preaching. Our God is a God of relationships—personal relationships!

I have shared my Beijing story with some of my friends over the years, and a few of them have chastised me for "compromising." I respectfully disagree with their point of view. It's easy to take personal beliefs and, like the Pharisees, impose those rules on everyone without regard for their cultural or social background. I am not talking about compromising the gospel or going against what the Bible explicitly teaches. I'm talking about our own set of values and mores that we establish for everyone to follow. Had I not been willing to temper my personal views, no relationship would have formed with my Chinese friends. I had to step out of my comfort zone and into their world to make that connection.

I don't want to make this lesson all about drinking. I firmly believe that drunkenness is prohibited in Scripture, and any amount of wine or alcohol could lead to unintended problems. I know many men and women who struggle with alcohol and rue the day they had their first drink. This and the possibility of causing a stumbling block for other Christians is more than enough reason for me to stay away from alcohol.

I guess the best way to encapsulate what I'm trying to say is to tell a story told to me by a pastor friend. A Southern Baptist Church sent a mission team to an Eastern European country to help a church they had partnered with. In preparation for their guests, the European church had purchased wine for their evening meals. These meals ended up being quite awkward as the mission team sat there and judged the European church members for drinking, while the European church members judged the women on the mission team for wearing makeup. Two different cultures collided, and I wonder how much mission work was accomplished!

Father, help us to see that You value people over our rigid rules and personal religious beliefs. We are reminded that it was the religious crowd who judged and crucified You because you often refused to bow to their petty religious rituals. May we not fall into the same trap of condemning others based on our legalistic views. Amen.

Eternal Significance

Do not store up for yourselves treasures on earth, where moths and vermin destroy, and where thieves break in and steal. But store up for yourselves treasures in heaven, where moths and vermin do not destroy, and where thieves do not break in and steal. For where your treasure is, there your heart will be also.
-Matthew 6:19–21

MOST OF US lead neatly compartmentalized lives. We have a material life filled with work, school, and family; then we have our spiritual life, which might involve a few hours at church on Sunday and perhaps a few minutes a day reading a devotional thought. Our two lives rarely intersect and are often diametrically opposed to each other. When a friend or acquaintance approaches us on the street, we are very adept at quickly figuring out which of the two personas we need to adapt and can change like a chameleon.

God never intended for us to live an uncomfortable, schizophrenic existence such as this, and it is a sure sign that our priorities are askew. Our material world of wealth, success, power, and comfort has become so important that many of us focus our efforts on them, with little thought of eternity. King Solomon, one of the wisest and wealthiest men in history, lived a significant portion of his life this way. What was his final observation? Solomon said,

> "After much thought, I decided to cheer myself with wine. And while still seeking wisdom, I clutched at foolishness. In this way, I tried to experience the only happiness most people find during their brief life in this world. I also tried to find meaning by build-

ing huge homes for myself and by planting beautiful vineyards. I made gardens and parks, filling them with all kinds of fruit trees. I built reservoirs to collect the water to irrigate my many flourishing groves. I bought slaves, both men and women, and others were born into my household. I also owned large herds and flocks, more than any of the kings who had lived in Jerusalem before me. I collected great sums of silver and gold, the treasure of many kings and provinces. I hired wonderful singers, both men and women, and had many beautiful concubines. I had everything a man could desire! So I became greater than all who had lived in Jerusalem before me, and my wisdom never failed me. Anything I wanted, I would take. I denied myself no pleasure. I even found great pleasure in hard work, a reward for all my labors. But as I looked at everything I had worked so hard to accomplish, it was all so meaningless—like chasing the wind. There was nothing really worthwhile anywhere" (Ecclesiastes 2:3–11).

Talk about regrets! This man had accomplished everything today's world deems valuable and successful. Yet as he looked back on his life, he had not accomplished anything worthwhile.

In 2008, I turned 50, the minimum age for retirement from the Secret Service. I knew I had many good years left and big plans for my professional future. But one particular day after reaching that milestone, I sat at my desk in the Chicago Field Office and considered how important temporal things had become to me. I had risen through the ranks of the Secret Service, had been a deputy assistant director, and was now the special agent in charge of one of the largest field offices in the Secret Service. I planned to transfer back to Washington, D.C., possibly as an assistant director. I was a driven person, and while many chase money and material wealth, I chased position, influence, and power. I had developed a great professional resume, but an honest inventory of my life showed very little in the area of eternal significance. I was storing up treasures on earth because that was where my heart was! I mulled it over for the next couple of days and weeks and found myself questioning why I even desired a higher position. To be honest, I didn't have a really good answer. I was a lot like John D. Rockefeller, who, at the peak of his wealth, was asked, "How much money is enough?" He answered, "Just a little bit more." At the time, his net worth was one percent of the entire economy in the United States. I called the director and told him I had decided to retire. He was surprised and asked me if I was leaving for another job. I told him I was not, but I felt it was just time to move on to another stage in my life.

The day after I retired, I picked up the Chicago newspaper to make sure Secret Service had not collapsed overnight because of my departure. It had not; in fact, the opposite was the case. The Secret Service had already named my replacement, and he was settling in "my" office.

As I drove out of Chicago to my new home in Mississippi, an incredible peace came over me. I didn't know where God was leading me, but I did know that wherever it was, I would start over with different priorities and a different view of eternity. Within 24 months, a chance encounter led me to work for the Billy Graham Evangelistic Association and Samaritan's Purse—two organizations that invest heavily in eternity. Finally, my life was balanced! I could enjoy the blessings of this world as God intended us to, but my focus was on Him and eternity.

The peace that comes from living life this way is incredible. Yes, I could have lived this way during my 25-year career with the Secret Service, and that would have been God's desire for me. But at some point, I lost perspective and, just like King Solomon, I got off track.

Solomon's final advice to us was this: "Don't let the excitement of youth cause you to forget your Creator. Honor him in your youth before you grow old and say, "Life is not pleasant anymore." Remember him before the light of the sun, moon, and stars is dim to your old eyes, and rain clouds continually darken your sky" (Ecclesiastes 12:1–2).

Lord, I pray we will take King Solomon's words to heart. As he lamented, it is dismal to get to the end of our lives and realize that we have nothing of eternal significance to show for our days on this earth. Many whom this world considers successful today will be paupers in eternity. Show us this reality and lead us to store up treasures in heaven where moths and vermin cannot destroy and thieves cannot steal. Amen.

Getting Off on a Technicality

---◆---

Then I saw a great white throne and him who was seated on it. The
earth and the heavens fled from his presence, and there was no place
for them. And I saw the dead, great and small, standing before the
throne, and books were opened. Another book was opened, which is
the book of life. The dead were judged according to what they had
done as recorded in the books. The sea gave up the dead that were
in it, and death and Hades gave up the dead that were in them, and
each person was judged according to what they had done. Then
death and Hades were thrown into the lake of fire. The lake of fire
is the second death. Anyone whose name was not found written in
the book of life was thrown into the lake of fire.
-Revelation 20:11–15

IN 1987, AS a young special agent assigned to the Ft. Worth office, I was given a
counterfeit currency investigation. Preliminary research into the history of these
particular $100 counterfeit notes indicated that they had first surfaced in Chica-
go, but recently hundreds of them had been passed in the Ft. Worth area.

I interviewed witnesses at numerous stores who had received these notes and
finally got a small break in the case. One of the store owners had suspected a $100
note she received might be counterfeit and wrote down the license plate number
of the man she thought passed the note in her store. It just happened to be an
Illinois license plate. I ran the plate number and found that the individual who
owned the vehicle had family in the Arlington, Texas, area. I drove to the family
member's address in Arlington, and sure enough, the Illinois vehicle was parked

in the driveway. I knocked on the door, and the gentleman who owned the car invited me in. I got all his personal information and then asked him about the counterfeit note that had been passed at the store. He admitted to stopping at the store to get gas but denied passing the $100 bill. He said he had used a $20 bill to buy gas and even produced a receipt verifying the purchase.

Sitting next to him was a briefcase, and I asked if he would mind if I took a look at its contents. He quickly denied my request. I asked him what was in the case, and he said it contained his wallet and other personal effects. Toward the end of the interview, I got a call on the radio from the office that the subject had a misdemeanor traffic warrant out for his arrest with the Arlington Police.

As I was leaving, I told him that I would like to drop him at the Arlington Police Department so that he could get the traffic warrant taken care of. He agreed, and I escorted him out to my car. Since the briefcase contained his wallet and personal effects, I grabbed it and put it in the trunk. When we arrived at the police station, I walked him to the desk sergeant and handed over the briefcase. The sergeant took him to the back office to fingerprint and process him while I went on my way.

As I was pulling out of the parking lot, a police officer came running to stop me. He breathlessly informed me that they had opened the briefcase to inventory the contents, and I needed to come inside to take a look. Back inside, the police officer opened the briefcase to reveal $50,000 in newly printed counterfeit $100 bills. We promptly arrested the man on federal counterfeit charges.

About two weeks after the arrest, I received notice of a court hearing before the federal judge in Ft. Worth. The purpose of the hearing was that the defendant and his attorney had filed a motion to suppress the counterfeit evidence found in the briefcase. I showed up at the hearing, fully confident that the motion would be thrown out. The motion to suppress was based on the fact that, as a federal agent, I had no authority to arrest the defendant on a misdemeanor state warrant. Had I not taken the defendant to the Arlington Police Department to take care of the traffic warrant, the briefcase full of counterfeit money would never have been discovered. To my utter amazement, the judge sided with the defendant and threw the counterfeit evidence out. I will never forget the smirk on the defendant's face as he looked at me and walked out of the courtroom a free man. Released on a technicality!

I tell this rather lengthy story to drive home a point regarding God's justice system. Our country's judicial system is heavily influenced by the philosophy that it is better that ten guilty go free rather than one innocent suffer, leading to a complicated system involving motions, hearings, discovery requests, and the endless search for a technicality or loophole. Many feel that this is how their judgment before God will take place. They think they will be able to bring proof of their good deeds, a church membership card, a baptism record, or a deacon ordination certificate to bolster their case. Elvis Presley famously wore a cross, the star of David, and the Hebrew letter chai, quipping, "I don't want to miss out on heaven due to a technicality."[13] But we will all appear before God with nothing in our hands. There will be no opening arguments, certification of evidence, cross-examination, or character witnesses. No chance to exploit a technicality or give an excuse. God will open the Lamb's Book of Life, and one of two judgments will be rendered: "Well done, my good and faithful servant" or "Depart from me, for I never knew you." Either your name is in the book, or it is not. Case closed, no appeals!

Father, thank You for the gift of Your Son and the resulting assurance we can have in our salvation. Thank You that Your system of justice is black and white without the constant stress of wondering if we have done enough to earn it. Because of Your Son's death on the cross, "not guilty" has already been stamped across our long list of sins. Because of that gift, may we strive every day to please You. Amen.

Don't Mess with My Logistics!

"For I know the plans I have for you," declares the Lord, "plans to prosper you and not to harm you, plans to give you hope and a future."
-Jeremiah 29:11

I WAS WORN out, sunburned from the Persian Gulf sun, and just ready to get home. I had been in Abu Dhabi for over a week preparing for former President Carter's visit to that country, and now that he had come and gone, all I could think about was getting home. My next destination was Cyprus for several days to visit my parents, who were Baptist missionaries to the Mideast, before flying home to the United States.

It was July 1990, and there was tension in the region because of Iraq's imminent invasion of Kuwait. I made sure to be at the airport in Abu Dhabi four hours early in case there were enhanced security procedures that I would need to navigate. Everything went smoothly, and I was soon settled in my seat, confident that I would make my connection in Dubai. And then the dreaded message came over the speaker system: "Ladies and gentlemen, we need everybody to disembark so we can do another security screening." Evidently, several pieces of luggage had been loaded on the plane that could not be associated with any of the passengers. We all got off the plane until they sorted everything out and reboarded one and a half hours later. By then, I knew I would miss my connection in Dubai.

When we landed in Dubai, I immediately got on the phone with the logistics desk for the Carter detail in Plains, Georgia, to see my options. The agent who ran the desk was efficient. If anyone could figure out how to get me to Cyprus and then home, he could. After all, he was always responsible for getting us where we needed to be, even in war-torn and third-world countries without commercial flights. He took pride in his job, and his favorite saying was, "Don't mess with my logistics!" He was sitting at a desk where he could see the big picture, and even though some of our logistical instructions sometimes didn't make sense, we knew he was on top of it. After about 30 minutes on hold, the agent came back on the phone and said, "Tim, I'm sorry, but we can't get you out for another two days. You'll need to stay put there in Dubai." As I hung up, I was not happy. Surely he had missed something. There had to be another way out!

I wandered over to the airline desk and got in line. When it was my turn, I explained my situation and asked the lady if she would check for options. She consulted her computer screen for several minutes and then slowly shook her head. "I just don't see anything," she said.

"Isn't there something through Europe or North Africa?" I asked.

"Well, there is one possibility—Syrian Air. But I don't know that I would recommend it."

I strolled over to the Syrian Air counter and noticed nobody in line, so I approached the desk. I handed them my ticket and explained that I was trying to get to Cyprus. The lady said, "Yes, we can get you there by tonight. We have a flight leaving in two hours to Damascus where you can connect with Cyprus Air to Larnaca."

"I'll take it!" I exclaimed, and she proceeded to handwrite a ticket for me.

One hour before the flight was scheduled to leave, an announcement came over the public address system announcing the gate number for my Syrian Air flight. I went to the announced gate and joined the other passengers waiting to board that flight. I did not see an aircraft parked at the gate, so I assumed it had not yet arrived. In a few minutes, the gate door to the outside opened, and a Syrian Air employee called for my flight number. The other 60 passengers and I followed him down a set of stairs to an old bus waiting for us on the taxiway. We climbed on the bus, which then headed for a remote part of the airfield where there was an old, dilapidated Russian-made aircraft parked out by itself. I got an uneasy feeling as we approached the aircraft and saw that there were no stairs at the front door, only a small set of steps that had been let down under the plane's tail. The bus pulled adjacent to the plane, and I saw our luggage sitting on the tarmac. The Syrian Air employee requested that before we boarded the plane, we go over and show the baggage handlers which bags belonged to each of us. Only after identifying our bag would they load them. It suddenly occurred to me that this was their baggage screening system. Anything left on the tarmac after everyone boarded the plane was considered suspicious and would be left behind. As we climbed the set of steps onto the back of the aircraft, we were all met at the top by the pilot, who frisked each passenger individually. My uneasy feeling had now turned into full-blown concern.

As we began to taxi, the whines and whirs commonly heard from an airplane's hydraulic system sounded more like a moan from an old bird that didn't feel like flying. As I looked around, I noticed the upholstery was worn and torn, and the pre-flight briefing did not include the instructions to bring our seatbacks to a fully upright position because half of the seats were broken and would not stay in that position. I was beginning to wish I had opted for the two-day stay in Dubai.

When the wheels finally touched down in Damascus, Syria, I felt such a sense of relief that I thanked the Lord over and over under my breath. I gathered my luggage and headed for the Cyprus Air desk. I had flown that airline before and knew they were a professional and well-run airline. I stepped up to the counter and presented the lady with my handwritten ticket that Syrian Air had issued. She looked at it for a moment, shook her head, and said, "We don't accept tickets from this airline." I explained my situation and that the original ticket was on Cyprus Air from Dubai to Larnaca, but I had missed my connection. She said she was sorry, but the ticket issued by Syrian Air was no good because they had trouble getting their money from that airline. "Besides," she said, "the flight to Cyprus was booked full, and the next flight was not for another two days."

I picked up my luggage and hurried to the Syrian Air ticket counter. To my dismay, it was closed, and nobody was there. I was in a real jam. I was traveling under a United States diplomatic passport, stuck in a country that the U.S. had declared a state sponsor of terrorism with no diplomatic relations, and nobody from my agency knew I was there. I couldn't leave the airport because I would have to go through their immigration checkpoint, and I didn't want the Syrians to know who I was or that I was there. I could hear the agent's voice on the Carter logistics desk: "Don't mess with my logistics!"

The simple definition of logistics is the planning and execution of a complex operation involving efficiently moving personnel or goods from one point to another. It is a term typically used in the military to describe the movement and housing of troops and their equipment. The key to a good logistical plan is that every step has been weighed and carefully thought out from the beginning of the mission through the end. God said, "'For I know the plans I have for you,' declares the Lord, 'plans to prosper you and not to harm you, plans to give you hope and a future'" (Jeremiah 29:11). God was delivering these words through Jeremiah to His people who were exiled in Babylon, but they are words that all of us who follow Him can claim. David said, "Your eyes saw my unformed body; all the days ordained for me were written in your book before one of them came to be" (Psalm 139:16). Both Jeremiah and David realized that God has a perfect logistical plan for every one of us, even before we are born. That plan involved where we were born, who our parents were, and what our talents and capabilities are. The problem is that once we start making our own decisions, our selfish wants, desires, and impatience affect that plan, and we either get in front of or ignore God's plan entirely. The results are often disastrous.

David was a perfect example of this. He was anointed king by Samuel when he was in his teens but didn't ascend to the throne until he was in his 30s. He spent much of his time living in caves and running from Saul, who was trying to kill him. Even though he had the support and admiration of Israel, he never got ahead of God's logistical plan. In fact, on two occasions, he had the opportunity to kill Saul and take the throne for himself, but he refused to deviate and continued his miserable life on the run. Had he decided to take things into his own hands, Israel would probably have ended up in a civil war between supporters of David and supporters of Saul. But because of his patience and sticking with God's plan, he became the greatest king Israel ever knew. How often do we grow self-centered and impatient and run after our desires without thought of God's plans for us? Financial gain, status, or popularity are all fool's gold if they are not in God's plan for our lives.

That night in Syria, I realized I had messed up by not sticking with the logistical plan of someone in the position to see the big picture. My strong desire to get home at any cost blinded me to the consequences of running off on my own. I returned to the Cyprus Air counter and implored them to find a way to get me on that flight. The lady again told me that there were no seats available. I told her that I would be close by in the gate area if anything came open and then sat and watched as passengers began to board the flight. Everyone was on board, and they were getting ready to shut the door when the gate agent motioned to me. She said they had one seat available, and if I would pay with a personal credit card, I could have that seat. I whipped out my card and gave it to her, not even asking her the price of the fare. I would have paid several thousand dollars to get on that plane!

I never doubted the agent on the logistics desk again. I might have some questions, and his instruction sometimes didn't make sense, but I trusted him to get me where I needed to be. In the same way, we must trust God and His logistics in our lives. Sometimes they may not make sense, but He sees the big picture. Don't mess with God's logistics!

Father, teach us to trust You. We know Your ways are perfect, but we tend to wander like sheep. Like sheep, we are easily distracted and chase after our own wants and desires. Help us to stay focused on You and Your will for our lives because true joy comes only from being in the center of Your will. Amen.

When God Is Silent

My God, my God, why have you forsaken me? Why are you so far from saving me, so far from my cries of anguish? My God, I cry out by day, but you do not answer, by night, but I find no rest.
-Psalm 22:1–2

KIDNAPPING WAS ALWAYS my significant concern for Samaritan's Purse employees, especially in some of the high-risk countries where we worked. As the head of security for the organization, it was my responsibility to ensure all our employees were prepared for such an event and that the organization had contingency plans in place and practiced them regularly.

We required all employees who would be traveling and working overseas to go through a three-day security course with high-stress practical exercises. During the kidnapping block, we put them through various role plays where they were held captive by instructors playing the part of hostage takers to practice what they had been taught in the classroom. These lessons involved what to say and do and what they shouldn't say or do in the presence of their captors. At the end of the block, we would discuss at length the organization's response if one of them was taken hostage.

We emphasized that in the event of a kidnapping, the international director of security and I would immediately travel, along with a crisis management team, to the immediate area where they were being held hostage. Even though the employee being held couldn't see or hear from us, they could be assured that we were close by. We told them we would shut down their social media accounts and keep the incident out of the media as much as possible to force the hostage-takers to deal directly with the crisis management team. We also told them that, eventually, the kidnappers would try to contact their parents or relatives, but their relatives would be told not to accept calls or communicate with the kidnappers, again, making them deal directly with the crisis management team. It would seem very quiet for them as a hostage— as if they had been abandoned. In fact, we told them that at some point, the hostage takers might come and tell them that nobody cared about them, but the contrary is true. I emphasized that we cared a lot about each of them, and even though it may seem very quiet to them, they should know that we were working day and night to gain their release. I promised them we would stay there as long as it took to win their freedom!

This is often what we as Christians feel like. We expect God to come riding in with the cavalry and immediately save us from a crisis. But often that is not how He works. We pray and pray, but all we get is silence. We begin to question whether God cares or is really there. Initially, our friends are there for us, but as the crisis drags on, they may get busy with their own lives, and again we're left alone. The silence is deafening!

The first thing we must realize is that God is near and He will never abandon us. He has promised that He will never leave us or forsake us. Psalm 139:7–12 says,

> Where can I go from your Spirit? Where can I flee from your presence?
> If I go up to the heavens, you are there; if I make my bed in the depths, you are there.
> If I rise on the wings of the dawn, if I settle on the far side of the sea, even there your hand will guide me, your right hand will hold me fast.
> If I say, "Surely the darkness will hide me and the light become night around me," even the darkness will not be dark to you; the night will shine like the day, for darkness is as light to you.

In our darkest times, we will have to take God's word for it. His promises are true, and even if we do not "feel" His presence, He is there. When I told the young employees in our security classes that if something happened to them, we would travel to their location and be close by, they believed me and took comfort in that. How much more comfort can we take in an omnipotent and omnipresent God who says He will always be near.

Second, just because God is silent doesn't mean our situation caught Him by surprise, and He is having to throw together a plan. The plan is already in place, but there could be several reasons for the apparent silence. He could be waiting for a change in our hearts or something we need to take care of. The Psalmist said, "If I had cherished sin in my heart, the Lord would not have listened" (Psalm 66:18). The only way to have an intimate, two-way conversation with God is to come before Him with a clean heart. He promises to draw near to us if we will draw near to Him (James 4:8). Or, it may be that He is speaking, but we are not listening or wanting to hear what He has to say. Sometimes, we are looking for what we think our answered prayer should look like and completely miss His perfect plan. Like Elijah, we may be looking for the wind, the earthquake, or the fire and miss the gentle whisper. Maybe God is silent because He knows we aren't ready for His message. We may need to go through trials before we're prepared to listen. Whatever the case, there is a reason for the silence. As I told the employees in security training, don't misunderstand the silence. There is a plan in place, and it is being carried out, even if you don't see its evidence.

Third, God will never walk away from you. The writer of Hebrews says, "God has said, 'Never will I leave you; never will I forsake you'" (Hebrews 13:5). God is going to stick with you until the end.

I once worked a kidnapping in the Mideast, where the individual was held for 120 days. We hung that individual's photo on our whiteboard in the Crisis Management Center as a constant reminder of why we were there. Day and night, we planned and strategized, constantly considering all options. During the day, we knocked on the doors of government officials, met with the U.S. Embassy, and collaborated with law enforcement and military officials. At night we wrote letters and emails and made phone calls. My first grandchild was born while I was there but leaving was not an option; I had given my word.

I love how the Amplified Bible states Hebrews 13:5: "He has said, 'I will never [under any circumstances] desert you [nor give you up nor leave you without support, nor will I in any degree leave you helpless], nor will I forsake or let you down or relax My hold on you [assuredly not]!'" God is near, He has a plan, and He will not walk away from us!

Lord, thank You for Your promise that You will never forsake us. May we lean on the assurance of Romans 8:28 and know that You are working things out for our good, even though it may seem quiet, and we may sometimes feel like our prayers are not getting through. Thank You that You are a Father who truly cares. Amen.

The Wiles of the Enemy

Be alert and of sober mind. Your enemy the devil prowls around like a roaring lion looking for someone to devour.
-1 Peter 5:8

THE RUSSIAN INVASION of Ukraine in February 2022 screamed across news headlines. Responses ranged from shock and disbelief to anger and panic. As I watched, I was drawn back to my trip with President Carter to Moscow in 1992, mere months after the fall of the Soviet Union. As the advance agent, I arrived several days early to make all preparations with the Russian Federal Security Service (formerly the KGB) for motorcades and security, in addition to coordinating the visit with the U.S. Embassy.

On the first day, I had a meeting at the U.S. Embassy. I arrived at the compound's front gate and met the Assistant Regional Security Officer (ARSO). As we walked across the complex, he pointed to the infamous, newly-built, eight-story U.S. Embassy Chancery that was supposed to be a state-of-the-art complex. Unfortunately, it could not be used because it was so full of Russian bugs and listening devices secretly installed by the Russian contractors who built it. The building had been completely gutted to no avail because many of the listening devices had been poured right into the concrete pillars that supported the structure. In addition to the bugs, the Russians had placed pipes, wrenches, unconnected diodes, and other metal junk in the concrete to frustrate any efforts to locate and remove bugs and listening devices. The U.S. government was now looking at what seemed the only option for the building—tearing it down and hauling it off.

As we walked to his office, the ARSO pointed out the large Russian church across the street from the embassy compound. On top of the church were clusters of antennas. He joked that they called it the Church of the Immaculate Reception. The story was that U.S. Ambassador Strauss would have to call the KGB from time to time, requesting that they turn down the microwave listening equipment due to embassy employees getting headaches. The ARSO made sure that I knew we would need to wait to have official conversations until we got to a "special room" deep inside the current embassy building. As we walked across the compound, I wondered how the U.S. government could have ever allowed the bugging of our new embassy right under our noses. Further, how could we trust the Soviets, much less consider them plausible friends? I soon found out the answer.

In December 1972, President Nixon was trying to curry favor with USSR Leader Leonid Brezhnev to get him to agree to come to Washington, D.C., for a summit. President Nixon got so caught up in trying to make the event happen that he lost all perspective and, over the state department's objections, signed an agreement allowing the Soviets to build the new United States embassy structure in Moscow in accordance with their codes and rules. He approved this arrangement even though the U.S. had found over 40 Soviet bugs hidden inside the walls of the former U.S. Embassy in 1964. They had been there for over a decade! Among other things, the agreement allowed the columns and beams to be pre-cast at a Soviet plant off-site and brought in by Soviet contractors. Rules were put in place that disallowed U.S. personnel from observing the process at the off-site plant. In essence, the new building was a Trojan horse.

So, where did President Nixon go wrong? First, he saw something he wanted so badly that he did whatever it took to get it. Second, he ignored previous experience and pushed the agreement through. Third, he disregarded the advice of experts who were very familiar with the enemy's tactics. Finally, and most egregiously, he trusted the enemy.

The Bible tells us how to deal with our enemy, the devil. James says, "But each person is tempted when they are dragged away by their own evil desire and enticed. Then, after desire has conceived, it gives birth to sin; and sin, when it is full-grown, gives birth to death" (James 1:14–15). This is how the enemy works. He dangles something in front of you that you know might be harmful. But the more you look at it, the more you want it, and you will soon do whatever it takes to justify it. Being tempted is not a sin. But if you allow your gaze to linger, as James says, it will become a desire. And that desire will eventually grow so intense that you will have difficulty rejecting it.

Once the enemy has instilled that desire in you, he will start the justification process. I'm sure President Nixon was well aware of our previous issues with the USSR. Still, he justified signing the embassy construction agreement for the "greater good" of our relationship with the Soviets. We can go back to the beginning to see how our enemy seeks to justify sin: "When the woman saw that the fruit of the tree was good for food and pleasing to the eye, and also desirable for gaining wisdom, she took some and ate it. She also gave some to her husband, who was with her, and he ate it" (Genesis 3:6). I can hear Eve's thought process: "Well, the fruit does look good, and I know that God wants us to be happy. Besides, what kind of loving God wouldn't want us to have more wisdom?" The serpent dangled the sin in front of Eve, her gaze lingered on the fruit, and then she justified it.

The enemy will always encourage you to ignore good counsel. Proverbs 12:15 says, "The way of fools seems right to them, but the wise listen to advice." The State Department dealt daily with the Soviets. They knew how cunning and ruthless they were. Yet President Nixon's ego led him to ignore their warnings. The Bible records the history of Israel's kings ignoring the prophets' warnings, and they suffered greatly for it. But let's bring it down to a personal level. How many people give us good counsel? Our pastor? Our youth pastor? Godly friends? What do we do when we are struggling with a decision we know may be wrong? We avoid them because we don't want to hear the truth. If we are in the process of making a life decision and don't want to seek any advice, we can be pretty well assured that we are on the wrong path.

Never trust the enemy. Jesus Himself speaks of the deceitfulness of the enemy. He says, "You belong to your father, the devil, and you want to carry out your father's desires. He was a murderer from the beginning, not holding to the truth, for there is no truth in him. When he lies, he speaks his native language, for he is a liar and the father of lies" (John 8:44). Lying is the enemy's principal weapon. He says that there is no God, the Bible is unreliable, there are many ways to God, and being good will get you to heaven. We sometimes like what he says, and it may even sound reasonable. But Paul says in 2 Corinthians 11:14 that Satan "masquerades as an angel of light," yet there is no truth in him.

Peter says, "Be sober [well balanced and self-disciplined], be alert and cautious at all times. That enemy of yours, the devil, prowls around like a roaring lion [fiercely hungry], seeking someone to devour" (1 Peter 5:8 AMP). This is a warning we all need to take to heart!

Father, give us wisdom in all we do because we are constantly being fed lies by the enemy. May we be forever wary of his attempts to distract and entice us. Give us strength to resist and quickly flee temptation. Help us surround ourselves with godly counsel and give us the prudence to listen to their advice and warnings seriously. Amen.

No Man Can Serve Two Masters

No one can serve two masters; for either he will hate the one and love the other, or he will be devoted to the one and despise the other. You cannot serve God and mammon.
-Matthew 6:24

THERE WERE 170 million stolen credit card and ATM numbers. The biggest financial fraud in history was committed right under our noses by someone we thought was on our side, whom we considered somewhat trustworthy.

It was 2003, and I was serving as a deputy assistant director for the Office of Investigations at Secret Service headquarters in Washington, D.C. As part of my responsibilities, I oversaw the operations of about 14 investigative field offices across the country.

One day as I was sitting in my office, I received a phone call from the special agent in charge of the Newark, New Jersey, office telling me that they had arrested an individual named Albert Gonzales on drug and credit card fraud charges. The charges carried an enhanced penalty because the drug violations occurred within a certain distance of an elementary school.

Through investigation into his background, they found that Albert was an up-and-coming administrator on the dark web for a cybercriminal group known as Shadowcrew. This group dealt in stolen identities, credit card numbers, and any other financial fraud they could profit from. Financial losses due to this group's activity were up in the millions of dollars. The Newark agent told me that Albert had agreed to help the Secret Service in its investigation into Shadowcrew in return for leniency on his drug and fraud charges.

We arranged for the Newark Field Office to rent space in a local warehouse for the undercover cyber operation. The investigation was dubbed *Operation Firewall*, and for several months, Albert Gonzalez, under the supervision of Newark agents, conducted business on the dark web with cybercriminals around the world. With Albert's help, agents collected massive amounts of evidence and intelligence while identifying numerous suspects and their locations. This continued for several months until we had enough evidence to indict and arrest 28 significant players. On the night the operation culminated, Secret Service agents simultaneously hit residences in eight states and six countries worldwide and arrested the cybercriminals. After all was said and done, 28 major suspects were arrested, and millions in losses were prevented.

Albert seemed to enjoy his newfound purpose with the Secret Service and continued to work with us in an advisory capacity, helping out where he could. He even traveled around the country with agents and spoke at seminars for banks and financial institutions, where he would share information on the techniques cybercriminals used to perpetuate their fraud. Albert had become a prized commodity for law enforcement in the fight against cybercrime.

Things appeared to be going well for Albert. Then in May 2008, a bombshell hit. Albert was arrested on charges of hacking into Dave and Busters and stealing 5,000 credit card numbers. After his arrest, investigative dots were connected. It was determined that he and several co-conspirators were also responsible for the TJX company hack, where they stole 45 million credit card and debit card numbers, and the Heartland Payment Systems hack, where 130 million credit card numbers were stolen—all while he was advising and working with the Secret Service and other law enforcement agencies! The lure of his old way of life was too great. It was rumored that he threw himself a $75,000 birthday party and complained that he had to count $340,000 in cash by hand because his cash counting machine had broken. At the time of his arrest, he had over $1,500,000 in cash and was staying in upscale hotels. Albert was convicted for his part in all crimes and sent to federal prison for 20 years.

Albert is a tragic example of how so many Christians choose to live. They hit bottom, cry out for the Lord, and are forgiven. They get a fresh start and realize the blessings of a new life. Yet the allure of the world and its materialism are too great. They try to live two lives—one life on Sunday and a different one Monday through Saturday. Jesus said, "No one can serve two masters; for either he will hate the one and love the other, or he will be devoted to the one and despise the other.

You cannot serve God and mammon" (Matthew 6:24). He didn't say it would be difficult to serve two masters; he said it is impossible! For a short while, it may appear to work. But at some point, one master will end up dominating your life at the expense of the other.

Paul puts it another way in Romans 6:16: "Don't you know that when you offer yourselves to someone as obedient slaves, you are slaves of the one you obey—whether you are slaves to sin, which leads to death, or to obedience, which leads to righteousness?" We are a slave to whatever influences us the most, whether it be our finances, entertainment, power, influence, or our relationship with God.

Matthew, Mark, and Luke record Jesus's interaction with the rich young ruler who came to Jesus and asked what he must do to inherit eternal life. Jesus gave him a list of commandments, and the young man said he was careful to keep them. Jesus then addressed the "other master": "You still lack one thing. Sell everything you have and give to the poor, and you will have treasure in heaven. Then come, follow me" (Luke 18:22). The young man left sorrowfully because he was very wealthy. Money meant more to him than anything else. Jesus gave him a choice between two masters, and he chose his wealth. How would we have answered the question? The true test is to honestly ask ourselves whether we could give up something if required by God. If not, we are trying to serve two masters!

Albert is a pretty extreme example of someone who tried to commit himself to two masters. He is currently learning a hard lesson about trying to play both sides. May we learn the same lesson before it is too late. God said, "Do not worship any other god, for the Lord, whose name is Jealous, is a jealous God" (Exodus 34:14). He takes a back seat to no person or thing. Along with Joshua, we need to say, "Choose you this day whom you will serve . . . But as for me and my house, we will serve the Lord" (Joshua 24:15).

Father, give us strength to resist as the things of this world constantly pull us. Your word says that money itself is not evil, but the love of money can quickly make it become our master. Forgive us when we put things before You. Help us to always desire You over "mammon." May our eyes always be set on eternity instead of just the pleasures of the here and now. Amen.

I Was Paid to Worry!

Who of you by worrying can add a single hour to your life? Since you cannot do this very little thing, why do you worry about the rest?
-Luke 12:25–26

MILLENNIALS ARE OFTEN referred to as the "Anxious Generation." In 2018, Pew Research polled 920 Generation X and Millennials and found that 70% of the respondents called anxiety and depression a "major issue" among their peers.[14] In a recent Harris Poll, 91% of Generation Z respondents reported feeling physical or emotional symptoms from stress.[15] But those of us from previous generations are just as bad!

For 25 years in the Secret Service, I was paid to worry. While making security advances for the president, I wouldn't sleep well for several nights leading up to his arrival, worrying that I had overlooked something. I kept a notebook on the nightstand because things would come to mind throughout the night, and I would get up and write them down so I would remember them the following day. Do I have the best motorcade and alternate routes? Do I know the way to all the hospitals along the way? Do I have safehouses designated? Have I met with all the appropriate law enforcement jurisdictions? Do I have enough magnetometers set up to handle the crowd? Have I allowed enough time for EOD (explosive) sweeps? These things and many more would rattle around in my head, making for restless nights.

In 2008, I was the special agent in charge of the Chicago Field Office with the Obamas living in my district. The Chicago Field Office was primarily responsible for the security of the first African-American presidential nominee in the history of this nation. This novelty brought added pressure, as I realized the severe implications for our country if anything happened to him. I kept my phone on vibrate next to my bed, jumping up to read any text or email that came in during the night. It was not a healthy way to live, physically or psychologically.

Unfortunately, these bad habits continued after I retired from the Secret Service. I always considered what could go wrong and took measures accordingly. It drove my wife and daughters crazy as I had them living in cocoons! I know several studies out there say 85% of the things we worry about never happen, but with my background, I felt that I needed to be closer to 100%! I guess I lived my life like the French philosopher Michel de Montaigne, who said, "My life has been filled with terrible misfortune; most of which never happened."[16]

Jesus said, "Who of you by worrying can add a single hour to your life? Since you cannot do this very little thing, why do you worry about the rest?" (Luke 12:25–26). The word translated *worry* or *anxious* in this passage means "to be torn apart." This is a great way to describe how worry affects us physically and emotionally. It is natural for us to be anxious or stressed from time to time. Whether we're speaking before a large group, participating in a sporting event, or taking a highly anticipated exam, our bodies naturally release cortisol. This stress hormone speeds up your breathing, raises your heart rate, and increases blood flow to the brain where you need it most. But what happens if the stress from your job, financial conditions, the constant bombardment of bad news, or family issues keeps you in a chronic state of worry and anxiety? Medical doctors tell us that it will eventually have a profound effect on you physically and emotionally in the form of heart palpitations, increased blood pressure, fatigue, depression, and irritability. This is the type of worry that Jesus is talking about in this passage, and it is destructive.

Once worry embeds itself in our minds, it deceives us into thinking things are worse than they are. What we need at these times is a little perspective. I can't tell you how often I have stayed awake worrying about something in the middle of the night, only to wake up the next morning and realize there was nothing to worry about once I could reason my way through it. Anxiety amplifies situations, and darkness always seems to make them worse.

The media doesn't help our inclination to worry. We have information overload through the news media and social media. Competition in these arenas today is fierce. The news media is all about ratings that produce profits. Much of what we hear from the news is exaggerated, sensationalized, targeted toward a particular demographic and narrative, and presented in a way to elicit strong emotions. This is the case whether it be Fox News, OAN, CNN, MSNBC, or any other network news station. I remember being at many events with the president or other world leaders, watching it later on in the news, and wondering if the media was at the same event I was.

Social media is just as damaging to our nation's anxiety problem. With Facebook, Twitter, Tik Tok, and Instagram, everybody has a voice, whether they are educated about what they are talking about or not. Misinformation is rampant on both ends of the spectrum. Reading from those platforms will increase anybody's anxiety level, no matter their political leanings.

Most importantly, worry and anxiety stunt our spiritual growth and reveal our faithlessness. How can we win a lost world when we are wringing our hands, worried about what will happen tomorrow? Jesus says, "And do not set your heart on what you will eat or drink; do not worry about it. For the pagan world runs after all such things, and your Father knows you need them" (Luke 12:29–30). When we are chronically anxious, we are acting like the pagan and unbelieving world.

My Achilles' heel for many years was anxiety. But in the last few years, I've made adjustments in my life that have saved me from this crippling spiritual disease. I share them with you only as suggestions:

- Spend time in the Word first thing in the morning before reading any news, looking at emails, or opening social media. I have a different outlook on everything after spending time with the Lord.
- Turn off the national news. I get my information from a news service that scans worldwide news and reports headlines from around the world. It comes by email every weekday morning, and I never spend more than fifteen minutes reading through it.
- Get rid of cable. My wife and I spend our time on streaming services watching old non-political sitcoms and shows without commercials. I've found that commercials can also invoke strong feelings and thoughts.
- Limit your time on social media and assume that most things you read are probably not entirely accurate. Use your social media account to keep up with friends and "unfollow" (not unfriend) those who want to bring up divisive issues constantly.

Remember, as followers of Christ, we live in a different reality from the rest of the world. Our reality is that we have a Father who cares for us and supplies our needs. Only we can claim the promise that "all things work together for good to them that love God, to them who are called according to his purpose" (Romans 8:28). If we genuinely believe that promise, our worries and anxieties will melt away.

Lord, we live in a noisy world that often tends to drown out what You are trying to say and do through us. Like Elijah, we are trying to hear Your voice through earthquakes, wind, and fire. No wonder we live in a state of anxiety and stress! Please help us to withdraw from the noise and listen for Your gentle and calming whisper. Only then can we see things from Your perspective, realize that You are in total control of everything in our lives, and know that You care and want the best for us. Amen.

A Wise King

---✦---

*So give your servant a discerning heart to govern your people and
to distinguish between right and wrong. For who is able to govern
this great people of yours?"*
-1 Kings 3:9

THIRTY-TWO DAYS away from home. I had been assigned to a "Jump Team"
of 15 agents who would support Vice President George H. W. Bush's final month
of campaigning before the election on November 8, 1988. We were put on an
Air Force C-141 cargo jet with the armored limos and Suburban follow-ups and
flown to whatever city the vice president would be campaigning in the following
day, never staying in a town more than two nights. Several times, we were stuck
on an airbase taxiway waiting to see where we were headed that day, and we often
didn't get to our hotel rooms until after midnight, with a report time of 6:00
a.m. the following day. I was tired, especially after spending the summer months
alternating between Democratic candidates Michael Dukakis and Lloyd Bentsen's
security details.

Election Day finally arrived, and we flew to Houston to work Vice President
Bush's election night watch party. We watched the results roll in all evening, and
the vice president was finally declared the winner around midnight. I dragged myself back to my hotel room, thankful for a soft bed, and planned to sleep in as long
as I could the following day. As I crawled into bed, I got a telephone call. President-elect Bush planned to be at his church first thing in the morning for prayer
before any other scheduled events. Out the window went my plans to sleep late!

Early the following day, we arrived at the Episcopal church. It was not a public or press event, just friends and family members. The pastor said a few words

and prayed, and then President-elect Bush stood to pray. I was struck that this was possibly the first time I had ever heard a public figure pray without a script or notes. As he prayed from his heart, it was as if he had just realized the enormous responsibility he had been given the night before. He prayed for wisdom, humility, and a servant's heart to humbly serve the people of this country. That was a moment I will never forget, and despite the lack of sleep, I am so thankful I witnessed it.

Just like President H. W. Bush, Solomon was overwhelmed when his father, King David, died and left him as successor to the throne. However, unlike President Bush, he was young and inexperienced. Unlike many brash young men who have come to power throughout history, he recognized that he was inadequate and needed God's assistance. Solomon prayed,

> Now, Lord my God, you have made your servant king in place of my father David. But I am only a little child and do not know how to carry out my duties. Your servant is here among the people you have chosen, a great people, too numerous to count or number. So give your servant a discerning heart to govern your people and to distinguish between right and wrong. For who is able to govern this great people of yours?" The Lord was pleased that Solomon had asked for this. So God said to him, "Since you have asked for this and not for long life or wealth for yourself, nor have asked for the death of your enemies but for discernment in administering justice, I will do what you have asked. I will give you a wise and discerning heart, so that there will never have been anyone like you, nor will there ever be. (1 Kings 3:7–12)

We can learn several things from this passage to ensure that we are all that God intends for us to be. First is humility. Solomon immediately recognized that he did not become king because of his talents and abilities. He was king because God had promised David his son would become king (2 Samuel 7:12–13). Solomon further acknowledged that he was young and inexperienced, a "little child," even though he was probably in his early 20s when he ascended to the throne. God loves humility; some of the most outstanding leaders this world has ever known have had this trait.

Second, Solomon asked for a discerning heart. While many will say this passage is about Solomon asking for wisdom, there is a difference between discernment and wisdom, even though they usually go hand in hand. Cambridge defines discernment as "the ability to judge people and things well," while wisdom is "the ability to use your knowledge and experience to make good decisions and judgments."[17] Solomon wanted to rule the people well, and discernment meant knowing right from wrong, understanding the motivations and hearts of his people, and doing right in God's eyes.

Last, Solomon realized what a great nation Israel was as God's chosen people, and he felt inadequate when he said, "For who is able to govern this great people of yours?" This was a rhetorical question because he realized that he could not do it without God's guidance. He had witnessed his father's reliance on God and knew it was the key to his success.

Solomon approached his new position as king with humility, a heart to serve his people well and do the right thing, and dependence on God. God was pleased with Solomon's requests because they were not self-serving; they came from a genuine motivation to lead the nation of Israel in a godly way. God blessed him with wisdom, discernment, wealth, and honor so that there was "no equal among kings."

Unfortunately, Solomon did not stay the course he set when he first became king. As time went by, he lost his humility when his wisdom became renowned, and his discernment vanished as he accumulated many foreign wives and allowed them to influence him. His material wealth became a god to him, and he burdened his people to support his lavish lifestyle. We don't hear much about Solomon during the last 10 years of his reign, but the book of Ecclesiastes details his somber regrets of misplaced priorities.

The prayer I heard in Houston, Texas, the morning after the election was similar to what Solomon prayed thousands of years ago. In fact, at his inauguration on January 20, 1989, President George H. W. Bush began his speech,

And my first act as president is a prayer. I ask you to bow your heads:

Heavenly Father, we bow our heads and thank You for Your love. Accept our thanks for the peace that yields this day and the shared faith that makes its continuance likely. Make us strong to do Your work, willing to heed and hear Your will, and write on our hearts these words: "Use power to help people." For we are given power not to advance our own purposes, nor to make a great show in the world, nor a name.

There is but one just use of power, and it is to serve people. Help us to remember it, Lord. Amen.[18]

President H. W. Bush began every cabinet meeting with prayer, which was always an essential part of his life. His self-deprecating humility was legendary, and he was always a favorite of all the agents and career mansion employees, from the chefs and maids to the White House butler. He even made it a point to stay at the White House through Christmas Day every year so that agents and staff could be at home with their families. He surrounded himself with wise advisors and sought spiritual counsel from his good friend Billy Graham. He displayed all the simple qualities that would have made King Solomon one of the greatest kings in history. Solomon should be a cautionary tale to each one of us. If we seek the qualities Solomon asked for and remain consistent in living them out, we will finish strong. If not, at the end of life, we will say with Solomon, "Vanity, vanity, all is vanity."

Father, give us discernment, wisdom, and humility as we walk with You. May we earnestly seek Your guidance in all that we do, and may we never forget that doing things in our own power and abilities will eventually lead us to pride, self-centeredness, and a total disregard for You. Amen.

The Earth Groans

We know that the whole creation has been groaning as in the pains
of childbirth right up to the present time.
-Romans 8:22

I HOISTED THE 50-pound bag of beans to my shoulder and walked slowly alongside the frail Haitian lady who had shown up at the food distribution site to get her food allocation. Most Haitian women carry impressive amounts of weight on their heads, and they could easily transport the bags of beans the 50 yards to where their families were waiting to assist them, but this lady needed help. She had received her supplies and was standing next to the back of the truck, wondering how she would get the heavy bags to her young grandson, who was waiting at the distribution site perimeter. She gladly accepted my offer of help, and we plodded along in silence until she pointed to a smiling nine-year-old boy waving to get her attention. As we got to the boy, he grabbed the bag of beans I was carrying and set them squarely on his head. The lady smiled and quietly thanked me before they turned and disappeared into the crowd. While it was a small deed, it gave me a sense of satisfaction mixed with the sadness of not knowing what would become of the woman and her grandson, whom I would never see again.

Many of us remember the catastrophic earthquake that hit Haiti on January 12, 2010. The videos on the news of the devastation and the heart-wrenching cries of the Haitian people looking for missing loved ones pulled at our heartstrings. After viewing one of these videos produced by Samaritan's Purse International Relief, I considered how I could personally get involved in the relief effort. At the time, I was retired and living in Madison, Mississippi, and I felt there was no reason I couldn't go and help in some way.

I contacted Samaritan's Purse and forwarded my resume to see what might happen. They quickly replied and said they needed a security manager to assist with their relief operations in Port Au Prince. After a few phone interviews and some paperwork, I was on a flight to Haiti.

I quickly settled into my job and took care of the immediate security needs at our base camp before focusing on our food distribution and shelter building operations. As in any situation where you have hungry and desperate people, safety and security issues must be addressed, especially at food distribution sites where large crowds could quickly overrun you. The overall crowd control was handled by the U.S. military and later by United Nations detachments from various countries. Still, the distribution plan had to be developed and implemented by Samaritan's Purse. This included handing out food coupons for specific sites and times to the women of each household who would show up for their rations on their designated day. Unfortunately, as in any disaster, we had our fair share of security incidents. On several occasions, our trucks loaded with beans and rice were hijacked on the way to the distribution site, and there was always the issue of stolen and counterfeited food coupons. There was never a dull moment, and every day brought a new challenge.

As with the elderly lady and her grandson, I enjoyed helping out with the food distributions when possible because it allowed me to interact with the Haitian people and remember why I was there. Their stories were heartbreaking, especially those of mothers who had sent their children off to school the morning of the earthquake and never saw them again. Everyone had a story about a missing husband, wife, family member, or friend.

I was amazed at the devastation as I drove through Port Au Prince. Buildings that had been four or five stories were now only eight or ten feet tall as the floors had "pancaked" down to the ground, crushing everyone in the building. Recovery efforts had slowed to a crawl, even though thousands of bodies were still in the rubble. Every day as I drove down Route 1 to the Samaritan's Purse base, I would pass by the town of Titanyen. I saw heavy machinery and dump trucks moving dirt up the hill beside the road. It was the site of the largest mass grave in Haiti, where most of the 220,000 bodies of people killed in the earthquake had been buried namelessly. Day and night for weeks after the quake, trucks full of dead bodies had brought their grisly cargo and dumped them in the trenches. Tents dotted the hillside as grieving family members had moved near the site to be "close to the spirits" of their deceased family members. As I observed all this suffering, I thought, "How could a powerful and loving God allow this to happen?"

To answer this question, we need to go back to Genesis and the fall of man. God said to Adam,

> "Because you listened to your wife and ate fruit from the tree about which I commanded you, 'You must not eat from it,' "Cursed is the ground because of you; through painful toil you will eat food from it all the days of your life. It will produce thorns and thistles for you, and you will eat the plants of the field. By the sweat of your brow you will eat your food until you return to the ground, since from it you were taken; for dust you are and to dust you will return" (Genesis 3:17–19).

Because of man's sin, the earth has been cursed. It is no longer the perfect creation we saw in the Garden of Eden and what God intended it to be. Because of this curse, man will always have to contend with "Mother Nature." Before his fall, Adam was the caretaker of a perfect garden. Now he would have to toil with the sweat of his brow, struggling not only with thorns and thistles but with droughts, floods, earthquakes, and the storms of a corrupted earth.

Paul said, "We know that the whole creation has been groaning as in the pains of childbirth right up to the present time" (Romans 8:22). In other words, all created things are suffering a shared misery because of the curse of sin. Women groan in childbirth, men groan as they toil, we all groan in sickness and disease, and the earth groans through nature and natural disasters.

So why wouldn't a loving God intervene in a situation like an earthquake in Haiti? Because He is a just and holy God who cannot tolerate sin. The curse on His creation was put in place because of Adam and Eve's sin and our continued rebellion against Him today, and we all live under it equally. Jesus Himself said, "He causes his sun to rise on the evil and the good, and sends rain on the righteous and the unrighteous" (Matthew 5:45). None of us are immune from this curse, which will continue until Christ returns and deals with sin for the last time.

But there is good news. All of us who are in Christ look forward to His return when we receive our new incorruptible bodies. Paul said, "For our dying bodies must be transformed into bodies that will never die; our mortal bodies must be transformed into immortal bodies" (1 Corinthians 15:53). No more sickness, disease, dying, or groaning!

At the same time, the curse on this earth will be lifted, and it will return to the way God intended it to be in the Garden of Eden. No more earthquakes, floods, droughts, hurricanes, or tornados. John said,

> "Then I saw 'a new heaven and a new earth,' for the first heaven and the first earth had passed away, and there was no longer any sea. I saw the Holy City, the new Jerusalem, coming down out of heaven from God, prepared as a bride beautifully dressed for her husband. And I heard a loud voice from the throne saying, 'Look! God's dwelling place is now among the people, and he will dwell with them. They will be his people, and God himself will be with them and be their God'" (Revelation 21:1–3).

A perfect world—so perfect that God will reside with us!

Father, thank You that You are a loving God who has provided a way of salvation. Let us fully realize that until You return, death is inevitable for all of us, whether by a natural disaster, accident, disease, or sickness, because we live under the curse of sin. With this in mind, help us live with an eye on eternity, not just the here and now. Amen.

A Serious Offense

So then, whoever eats the bread or drinks the cup of the Lord in an unworthy manner will be guilty of sinning against the body and blood of the Lord.
-1 Corinthians 11:27

SUNDAYS AT THE White House when President and Mrs. Clinton were in residence were quiet and routine. The president and first lady usually attended church at Foundry Methodist and then came back to the White House for lunch or went out to eat unexpectedly—causing total chaos for the restaurant. These impromptu restaurant visits were "off-the-record" movements for which we weren't too concerned about advanced security arrangements. If it was not on his schedule and only we knew where the president would show up, there was very little chance someone wanting to do him harm could ever plan on his being there.

On the other hand, his church attendance was always considered "on the record" because the president usually attended when he was in town. This meant a security advance team had to be at the church early before anyone arrived to start the security sweep and post agents around the facility. As the congregation arrived, they were required to go through metal detectors as they entered the auditorium. This had become routine for the attendees, and most accepted it, knowing it was the price they paid for attending the same church as the president.

We usually arrived with the president and first lady five minutes before the service started. They were escorted to the front of the church, where there were several rows roped off for them and their senior staff. Agents were scattered throughout the congregation, with the presidential detail leader and the first lady agent sitting directly behind the Clintons.

This had become routine, and because I was "on duty" and not an active participant in the service, it was never a worshipful experience for me. This, coupled with the fact that I was going through a dry period in my spiritual life, made for a dead religious experience. The long hours, constant travel, stress, and feelings of self-importance had sucked the spiritual life out of me. It was as if I was living in Ezekiel's valley of dry bones, longing for a spiritual breath to once again fill my life.

One such Sunday morning, while I was assigned to the first lady detail, I accompanied President and Mrs. Clinton to church. As we arrived, I followed Mrs. Clinton down the aisle and took my place behind her in the pew. That particular morning, communion was scheduled, and after a brief sermon, people were invited to file to the front of the church row by row to take a wafer from the pastor and drink from a common cup. When it came time for his row, President Clinton stepped out with his two agents, and they went forward, and all three took the elements. Mrs. Clinton stepped out next, and I dutifully followed her down the aisle to the front of the church so that I could be in close proximity. She took the elements, and then it was my turn. Suddenly, an overwhelming feeling of guilt welled up inside of me, and I took a step back, letting the people behind me go ahead while I followed Mrs. Clinton back to her seat. All I could hear in my head was the scripture my father, a pastor, always quoted before administering the Lord's Supper: "So then, whoever eats the bread or drinks the cup of the Lord in an unworthy manner will be guilty of sinning against the body and blood of the Lord" (1 Corinthians 11:27). If there ever was anyone this was directed at, it was me!

The New Testament church in Acts often ate meals together. The rich and the poor would come together, bringing what they had and sharing their food equally. At the end of their meal, they would have communion, where they would partake of the wine and the bread, remembering what Christ had done for them on the cross. The Corinthian church had taken this practice and turned it into a travesty. The rich would come and gorge themselves with each other while the poor stayed to themselves and went hungry. When it came time for communion, some of the rich were often drunk and certainly not in the right frame of mind to observe the Lord's Supper. Communion was supposed to be about the church's unity, but they had turned it into a meaningless and divisive sacrament. Paul told them that if they were hungry, they should eat at home so that when they met for the Lord's Supper, they would be reverent and focused on its true meaning.

After Paul explained what the Lord's Supper should not be, he warned them about taking communion unworthily or in the wrong frame of mind. He says, "Everyone ought to examine themselves before they eat of the bread and drink from the cup" (1 Corinthians 11:28). This examination has two parts. First, we should never partake while we have unconfessed sin in our lives. Second, we should enter into the time with reverence and reflection on Christ's sacrifice for us. This time of reflection is necessary because it makes us keenly aware of our sinful state and drives us to the forgiveness that only the cross can offer.

Often, the Lord's Supper is tacked on to the end of the service without allowing proper time for this preparation. Paul warns that when we do this, we are "sinning against the body and blood of the Lord." In other words, we are sharing in the guilt with those who actually carried out the crucifixion of Jesus! This should give us pause to think before we flippantly enter this holy time of remembrance.

Paul takes it a step further when he says, "For those who eat and drink without discerning the body of Christ eat and drink judgment on themselves" (1 Corinthians 11:29). Because of the way the Corinthians defiled the table of the Lord, there were some who were weak, sick, and even dead. This was probably a judgment specific to the Corinthian church, but it emphasizes for us the seriousness of taking communion lightly.

Being raised to know the significance of the Lord's Supper is what caused me to withdraw from participating in communion on that Sunday back in 1995. I'm sure anyone who might have seen me refuse the elements assumed I was a heathen and an unbeliever, but the opposite was true. I was convicted of unconfessed sin before a holy God and refused to make a mockery of the Lord's death. It was through this conviction that my dry bones began to come alive again. This is the purpose of the Lord's Supper: to bring us to confession and remind us of the gracious work Christ did for us on the cross. Without these two acts, we are guilty of "sinning against the body and blood of the Lord," a serious offense.

Lord, may we always come to Your table with clean hearts and a sense of awe for what You did for us on the cross. May it never become routine or mundane but allow it always to be a fresh reminder of the price You paid for our redemption, a priceless gift that we could not purchase ourselves. Amen.

Refusing to See the Truth

Anyone who chooses to do the will of God will find out whether my teaching comes from God or whether I speak on my own.
-John 7:17

SHE WAS AN elementary school reading teacher we arrested for passing counterfeit $100 bills at the local Walmart. This was a new one for me because she didn't fit the typical profile of a counterfeiter. But as the evidence mounted, there was no doubt in my mind that she had knowingly committed the crime for which she was arrested.

The investigation started when the Secret Service office in Shreveport, Louisiana, received reports of counterfeit $100 bills being passed in a small town in northern Louisiana. A break in the case came when a Walmart loss prevention manager called and said that five of these particular counterfeits had been passed by a customer at one of their cash registers the previous day. He said they might have some video footage of the transaction, so I headed to the small town to see what I might find.

When I arrived, the manager had already reviewed the video and identified the suspect. He told me that the cashier who accepted the five fake bills had been suspected of stealing from the cash register. Unbeknownst to her, the store installed a special video camera above her register to record her actions. The video camera had captured the transaction as an area schoolteacher passed the five counterfeit bills to the suspected cashier, who just happened to be her sister-in-law.

As I watched the video, I saw the teacher approach her sister-in-law's register and get in line behind several other customers, even though other lines were open and without a wait. She had only eight small items in her basket, and when it was her turn to check out, she placed two articles on the counter and pulled out a $100 bill to pay for them. The cashier gave her the change, after which she put two more items on the counter and pulled out another $100 bill. She did this four times, each time paying for two small things with a $100 note. After receiving the change from the fourth bill, she looked in her basket and saw that she did not have any more merchandise, so she reached over and grabbed a Nutrageous candy bar from the rack next to the cash register and paid for it with a fifth bill. After getting the change from the fifth bill, she gathered her items and left.

I took custody of the video, thanked the loss prevention manager, and headed to the local police department to try to track down where the suspect lived. Since it was a small town, they quickly identified who it was and gave me her home address. I found the house, knocked on the door, identified myself, and asked if we could talk. At first, she denied passing the notes at the Walmart, but when presented with the evidence, she admitted buying some items with the five bills, though she denied knowing they were counterfeit. When I asked who had given her the notes, she claimed she had received them when she cashed a check at the local bank. I asked her why she made five different transactions, and she said she was buying for five other family members and needed five separate receipts. I showed her copies of the five receipts I had obtained from Walmart, and the total of all five was less than $20. I asked why she couldn't have conducted all five transactions from the change she received from the first bill. She shrugged and said she did not have an answer to that. I confirmed all her personal information, including that she was a local elementary school reading teacher, and told her I would get back in touch.

I went directly to the bank, where the suspect claimed to have cashed the check and received the five bogus bills. As expected, there was no record of any such transaction between the suspect and the bank.

The following week, I presented the case to the United States Attorney's Office in Shreveport for the prosecution of the suspect on federal counterfeit charges. She was indicted by a federal grand jury several weeks later. After reviewing all the evidence in the case, the federal prosecutor fully expected a plea agreement before the case ever went to trial, as happens in the majority of cases. But not this one. The suspect probably reasoned that her teaching career would be over if she pleaded guilty to counterfeiting charges, so she decided to roll the dice and go to trial.

Several days before the trial, a jury selection took place. Among the jurors selected were several school teachers, which the Assistant U.S. Attorney thought was positive. Surely these teachers would be incensed at one of their own smearing the reputation of such an honorable profession and vote to convict her.

As the trial started, the central piece of evidence, the Walmart video, was shown in the courtroom. The jury members watched intently, and several snickered a little when the defendant looked around and grabbed a Nutrageous candy bar, and paid for it with her last counterfeit bill. The fact that the camera was in place because of her sister-in-law's dishonesty and that she insisted on going through that particular line, even though there were other lines open, were points emphasized by the prosecutor. I took the stand and testified that her actions were typical of someone passing counterfeit as she repeatedly purchased small items with large counterfeit notes to receive genuine currency as change. I also testified that she lied to me about where she had gotten the notes.

When the defendant took the stand, she claimed that she must have been mistaken about where she received the notes and now couldn't remember where she got them. She was also fuzzy on what items from her shopping cart she was buying for which family members. During the entire trial, the two teachers in the jury sat stone-faced. It was impossible to read what they might be thinking.

The trial ended, and we thought the jury deliberation would take an hour, two hours at most. However, nothing came back that afternoon, so we went home thinking we would hear something the following morning. The next day came and went with no news from the jury, even though they sent several questions about the evidence to the judge and asked to see the video again. I wondered what was taking the jury so long. The Secret Service had a 97 percent conviction rate, and I had never had a counterfeit case with more damning evidence against the defendant. That afternoon, we went home, still not having heard anything.

Finally, on the third day, we got the news that there would be no conviction because the jury was hung. Despite all the evidence, the teachers refused to vote to convict, even though all the other jury members were sure of the defendant's guilt. They had shown up for the trial believing there was no way one of their own would commit such a crime, and no facts or evidence would change their minds.

This is a significant problem in our society today, even for those of us who call ourselves Christians. There is no searching for absolute truth. We are firmly planted in what we believe and have closed our eyes and ears to any facts or reasoning that might jeopardize our beliefs. Someone gave me some humorous aviation clichés written by pilots a while back, and one of them said, "If you're ever faced with a forced landing at night, turn on the landing lights to see the landing area. If you don't like what you see, turn 'em back off." That seems to be how we fly today. Often the truth is bothersome, so we choose to ignore it. The Gospel of John often refers to Jesus as the light of the world. John says, "This is the judgment, that the Light has come into the world, and men loved the darkness rather than the Light, for their deeds were evil" (John 3:19). Just like the airplane landing lights, if we don't like the truth we see in the light, we snuff out the light and choose to live in darkness. This is why the religious leaders plotted to get rid of the light: He was an inconvenient truth.

Jeremiah ran into this same thing as he addressed a sinful and corrupt Israel. He said, "Hear this, you foolish and senseless people, who have eyes but do not see, who have ears but do not hear" (Jeremiah 5:21). John Heywood paraphrased this verse perfectly in 1546 when he said, "There are none so blind as those who will not see."

The Pharisees and religious leaders in Jesus's day knew what they wanted the Messiah to look and act like and refused to see the truth of the prophecies concerning Jesus. Only Nicodemus was honest enough to approach Jesus and search out the truth, even at the risk of knowing it might rock his world and change his belief system. Jesus challenged the religious leaders when He said, "Anyone who chooses to do the will of God will find out whether my teaching comes from God or whether I speak on my own" (John 7:17). He wasn't telling them to accept what He was saying by blind faith. He was telling them to test what He was saying and make a personal commitment to the truth, no matter where it took them. Throughout history, men have accepted Jesus's challenge, and the changes in their lives have been remarkable.

Lew Wallace was indeed a talented man—a writer, artist, and prosecuting attorney. He fought in the Mexican-American War and the Civil War, becoming the youngest major general in the Union Army. He was an agnostic who had no convictions about God or Christ. One day he encountered well-known atheist Robert Ingersoll. Instead of just accepting Ingersoll's version of the truth, he decided to investigate the Bible himself. His research resulted in his becoming a follower of Christ and writing *Ben Hur: A Tale of the Christ,* the best-selling novel of the 19th century.

Such was also the case with C. S. Lewis, a former atheist. Through his honest research and studying of the Bible, he first became a theist and, soon after that, a follower of Christ and one of the greatest Christian writers of the 20th century. As Jesus said, the truth is there if you honestly search for it.

The problem is that Christians can be just as bad as the world at turning off the light of truth and living in our comfortable reality. We have become intellectually lazy and, like the Pharisees, have established what we believe, and nobody will move us off that hill. We have stopped searching for truth in God's Word and rely on what we learned as young and immature Christians. The writer of Hebrews says, "For the word of God is alive and active. Sharper than any double-edged sword, it penetrates even to dividing soul and spirit, joints and marrow; it judges the thoughts and attitudes of the heart" (Hebrews 4:12). God's Word is unlike all other books. The more you study God's Word, the more truth will be revealed. We may not like what the light of truth exposes, but conviction is part of sanctification, pressing on toward the goal of Christlikeness. If we are not searching for truth and adjusting accordingly, we are just like those teachers on the jury who were not going to allow any amount of evidence or truth to jeopardize their beliefs. There are none so blind as those who will not see!

Father, open our eyes to Your truth. Search us and bring to light things in us that need to change. May we be open to Your Spirit's prompting and correction, and may we never stop working out our salvation until we are finally at rest with You. Amen.

Servant Leadership

For even the Son of Man did not come to be served, but to serve, and to give his life as a ransom for many.
-Mark 10:45

AS I WENT through management and leadership classes in preparation for my senior executive appointment with the Secret Service, I studied the leadership styles of military and political leaders throughout history. Each had their own style, some were successful and others failed. The one who intrigued me the most was Alexander the Great, who exploded onto the world scene in 336 B.C. at 20 years old and conquered a large part of the known world before his death at 32. Alexander was sometimes paranoid, egotistical, and morally bankrupt, but one aspect of his leadership style that made him successful was his philosophy of servant leadership. He quickly found that this quality endeared him to his men, promoted loyalty, and explained why his army was willing to go on a military campaign for 10 consecutive years and cover over 10,000 miles.

Alexander maintained the same accommodations as his men, living among them in a tent just like theirs. He shared the discomforts of the cold, heat, and hunger. While many generals throughout history would position themselves at the rear of the front lines, Alexander always fought at the front, visible to his men. He was trained as a doctor and used his skills to treat and give medical assistance to his soldiers. He was wounded numerous times, three of which were almost fatal, yet he refused treatment until all other injured soldiers were cared for. Most impressively, he made a point to know the names of at least 10,000 of his soldiers.

Alexander allowed his men to share in the plunder as they conquered city after city. By the time they reached present-day Afghanistan, it is said that they had an extra wagon train to carry all that his army had pilfered. This became a problem as their accumulated treasures began to severely hamper their mobility. Their mobility was the key to making them so effective. Alexander finally assembled his men and explained that their plunder was slowing them down. At the conclusion of his compelling speech, Alexander took a torch and burned all of his wagons containing the treasure he had accumulated. Inspired by their commander, his men set their wagons with their prized possessions on fire.

Alexander the Great was complex, and his leadership was often incongruent with his other actions. I don't know if his leadership style was out of genuine concern for his men or if he stumbled onto the servant leadership model and found it worked. Either way, this form of leadership was taught and emphasized repeatedly by Jesus. John 13:3–17 records Jesus washing the feet of his disciples. They had gathered in the upper room the night of the Last Supper, and with all the jostling for position and rank, none of the disciples had even considered undertaking the job that was usually the task of a servant. The lesson that Jesus taught them that night was indeed a lesson we all need.

How ashamed His disciples must have initially felt when Jesus got down on His knees to do the work of a servant. But Jesus did not mean to shame them; He wanted to show them how much He valued, loved, and appreciated them. How many CEOs in this world go to these lengths to show appreciation for their line employees? If they did, they would have fewer disgruntled workers and union problems. Everyone needs to feel appreciated and valued.

Jesus didn't just lecture them; He modeled His own teaching. So many leaders today have the attitude, "Do as I say, not as I do." If leaders are unwilling to do what employees do, expect dissension in the workforce. Because Jesus modeled it, He had every right to expect His disciples to "wash each other's feet." At the White House, I had two supervisors volunteer to work Christmas Day because they knew several of us had young children. They were willing to take the early morning shift on Christmas morning to allow us to be with our children. That impacted me greatly and encouraged me to want to do the same for others in return.

Jesus could wash their feet because He knew who He was. The Creator of the universe knew that doing a menial or distasteful task did not diminish who He was or lower His standing. Servant leaders find that acts of kindness endear them to their employees. Insecure leaders are wrapped up in titles, positions, and exclusivity, fearing that any crack in that facade portrays them as weak and ineffective.

The account of Jesus washing the disciples' feet was just a precursor to Jesus's ultimate act of servitude. The next day, He willingly laid down His life for all who call Him Lord and Master. The Gospel of Mark says, "For even the Son of Man did not come to be served, but to serve, and to give his life as a ransom for many" (Mark 10:45). If Jesus was willing to do this for us, why wouldn't we be willing to have a servant's heart for all, even those who call us boss?

Father, we are so proud and egotistical. The more status we gain, the less we are willing to serve but rather demand service from others. Convict us of our arrogance. Forgive us when we consider serving others beneath us. May we always remember and emulate your humility and meekness. We pray that you would give us all servant's hearts like Yours. Amen.

No Insignificant Job

Just as a body, though one, has many parts, but all its many parts
form one body, so it is with Christ. For we were all baptized by one
Spirit so as to form one body—whether Jews or Gentiles, slave or
free, we were all given the one Spirit to drink. Even so the body is
not made up of one part but of many.
-1 Corinthians 12:12–14

U.S. SECRET SERVICE recruiting posters show photos of young stern-looking men and women walking or running next to the president's limo or working him through a rope line. They portray the Secret Service as a genuinely glamorous, prestigious job. While that is partially true, in reality, for every one of those agents you see publicly or on television, nine others are working behind the scenes to ensure the president's safety.

I became painfully aware of this right after I was hired. The 1984 Republican Convention was in Dallas, Texas, where I was assigned. I had completed the first part of my training but was back in Dallas for a month waiting for the second school. Since I was a warm body, I was pressed into service with the transportation section for the convention. The agency brought in about 35 leases for follow-ups, limos, and motorcade vehicles for the president and vice president. They were secured in an outdoor parking lot in downtown Dallas. My job for three weeks was to ensure those cars were gassed, washed at an area carwash, and ready to go each time they were used. During those three weeks, I washed and gassed over 100 vehicles. I don't remember the Secret Service ever advertising car maintenance on the recruitment posters. Still, I could take pride in knowing not a single car in the president's motorcade ever ran out of gas.

Once fully trained, I was often sent to President Reagan's ranch in Santa Barbara, California, when he was there to vacation and take some time off. They usually posted me a ways from the president's house among the trees and brush to ensure nobody compromised the outer perimeter. Except for a few breaks during the day, I was out there for 12 hours watching for something that never happened, still not appearing in any of those photos advertising the Secret Service.

And I will never forget the many hours I spent standing in hotel stairwells on the president's floor while he slept. Or the time I was posted on the roof of the Century Plaza Hotel in Los Angeles all night to make sure nobody had access to the hotel air intake. Such was the life of a young agent who could only dream of one day being on the presidential detail and living the glamorous lifestyle.

Later in my career, my whole perspective changed as I gained more experience and eventually made it to the presidential detail. I finally realized that the most essential part of protecting the president was taking place in those seemingly insignificant assignments away from the limelight.

A good security plan has three rings of security: the outer, middle, and inner. The inner ring is what gets attention. However, the real protection of the president takes place in the middle and outer perimeters, at checkpoints, magnetometers, and barriers a distance away from the president. If a threat got through those two outer rings of security, the odds of the inner perimeter being able to neutralize an attacker before he strikes are not great. Yet the critical jobs of those serving in the less desirable places go unnoticed and underappreciated. I have never had anyone ask me to tell them the story about the time I stood on a smelly loading dock at the president's hotel for 10 hours. They much prefer to hear my stories of being close to the president.

In the body of Christ, the preachers, worship leaders, singers, and teachers are the face of the church. Their photos are on the church's website and other media. What you generally don't see are the photos of those praying alone in the prayer room, visiting the hospitals, changing diapers in the nursery, or cleaning tables after a fellowship supper. But if those people weren't doing the "menial" jobs, the church would not be the church. Paul addresses this when he says, "The eye cannot say to the hand, 'I don't need you!' And the head cannot say to the feet, 'I don't need you!'" (1 Corinthians 12:21).

Throughout the book of 1 Corinthians, Paul corrects many harmful attitudes that had crept into the church. It was a diverse church of wealthy Greeks and

Jews, along with indentured servants and slaves. But instead of all these groups being united in Christ, divisions had grown between the different factions. In the previous chapter, Paul chastised the wealthy for gorging themselves during the Lord's Supper while the poor went hungry. Now he had to address the pride and arrogance regarding the gifts and position. The church had talented teachers and leaders, but their pride had caused them to look down on those they considered to have lesser tasks and responsibilities.

Paul used the analogy of the body to show that every part is unique with a different purpose, yet every member is vital to the proper functioning of the body. If one part is missing or maimed, the entire body suffers and cannot reach its potential. Conversely, it is only through our recognition of diverse gifts that we can have complete unity in the church. Imagine a church in which everyone had the gift of teaching, but no one had the gift of service or hospitality. It would be a dysfunctioning body doomed to failure!

Paul continues: "On the contrary, those parts of the body that seem to be weaker are indispensable, and the parts that we think are less honorable we treat with special honor" (1 Corinthians 12:22–23). While the world honors those out front and visible, Paul says it is the ones operating behind the scenes and in less honorable positions that are indispensable. Like everything else in the gospel, this is upside down in the world's eyes.

Later in my career and as a supervisor, when the president came to my district, I always took time to walk around some of the outer posts and talk to the young agents assigned responsibilities away from the action to let them know they were appreciated and that what they were doing was essential to the mission. No matter how insignificant they thought their role was, the overall security plan would be full of holes without them. It is the same with the body of Christ. Every one of us is crucial to the church's mission, no matter how mundane we may think our contribution is. Without each of us exercising our gifts, the body will never be complete and functioning to its potential. Just as the human body has no extra parts that serve no purpose, so it is with the body of Christ. There are no spectators, only participants.

Father, each of us has specific skills and talents we should utilize for Your kingdom. May we use these abilities to build up the body of Christ, no matter how insignificant we may feel they are. We are reminded that just like the fish and loaves of bread, You can take seemingly small things and use them in powerful ways if we only make ourselves available. Amen.

The Race

Brothers and sisters, I do not consider myself yet to have taken hold of it. But one thing I do: Forgetting what is behind and straining toward what is ahead, I press on toward the goal to win the prize for which God has called me heavenward in Christ Jesus.
-Philippians 3:13–14

THE BAKER TO Vegas Challenge Cup is a 120-mile law enforcement relay race every spring. It starts in the Mojave Desert at Baker, California, often called the "Gateway to Death Valley," and ends in Las Vegas, Nevada. Law enforcement teams made up of 20 runners come from all over the nation and the world to compete for the coveted trophy and bragging rights for the following year. It is a grueling race, with each stage or leg averaging six miles through the blazing desert sun and climbing from a 900-foot elevation to the highest point of 5,600 feet at Mountain Springs Pass. As the sun goes down, temperatures dip, sometimes into the 30s, as the race continues overnight and into the next day. Each team has a follow-up vehicle with water, supplies, and support personnel urging the runners on.

Every year, the Secret Service office in Los Angeles fields a team for the race. In 1998, I was new to the office and thought it would be fun to experience it, so I went out and ran the five-mile qualifying trial through the flat streets of Los Angeles and finished in the top 20, earning me a place on the team. Over the next several months, I trained hard, running the hills in Riverside where we lived, and trying to acclimate to the hot, arid weather. As the race drew closer, the team captain called and asked which leg of the race I would be interested in running. Not overly fond of running in extreme heat, I asked for one of the later legs to run at night. He assigned me one of the stages at which I would get the baton at one

221

or two in the morning. The downside was that most of my leg would be primarily uphill.

The day of the race, I slept a couple of hours that evening, and then made my way to the staging area close to the point where I would receive the baton. It was after 10 p.m., cold, and windy. The night was dark except for the flashing blue lights of the follow-up vehicles, as far as the eye could see, slowly trailing their runners. Some of the better teams whose runners constantly train for the race had passed 45 minutes earlier, and from the information I received, there were probably at least 30 teams ahead of us.

Eventually, my teammate and our follow-up vehicle came in sight, and I stood up, did a few last-minute stretches, and got ready to take the baton. As he got closer, I could see the pained look on his face, and as he handed me the baton, he collapsed next to the road, completely worn out from giving everything he had. Baton in hand, I started the gradual incline that I knew would increase the further I went. Sure enough, a mile into my run, the terrain became noticeably steeper. At the three-mile mark, I was really beginning to labor. While a few runners passed me, I started to pass others who had slowed to a jog or walk. Others had even stopped beside the road and were bent over, trying to catch their breath. By the fifth mile, I was struggling and beginning to wonder if I would make it. The encouragement coming from the follow-up car was all that kept me going. Then something amazing happened. I came over one last steep ridge, and there on the horizon was the glow from the city of Las Vegas! The terrain somewhat leveled out, and I got a fresh surge of energy. The finish was still 40 miles away but at least in sight. I finished up my leg, handed the baton off to the next runner, and bent over to catch my breath, satisfied that I had done my very best and eager to head toward those lights where I would find a soft hotel bed and some rest.

The writer of Hebrews compares our lives to a race when he says, "Therefore, since we are surrounded by such a great cloud of witnesses, let us throw off everything that hinders and the sin that so easily entangles. And let us run with perseverance the race marked out for us" (Hebrews 12:1). Who are these witnesses? They are the heroes of the faith mentioned in chapter 11: Abel, Enoch, Noah, Abraham, Isaac, Jacob, Sarah, Joseph, Moses, Rahab, David, and Samuel, to name a few. I don't think they are sitting in heaven watching us run the race, but with the image presented, they are the ones who ran before us and then handed the baton off to us. We should honor how they ran the race by putting as much effort into running our leg as they did. Just as the other 19 runners on my team cheered for and depended on me to do my part, these heroes of the faith are doing the same.

The passage says, "And let us run with perseverance the race marked out for us." God assigns which course we will run. It may be uphill, downhill, in extreme heat, or in freezing cold. Every one of the heroes of the faith ran a completely different leg, some much easier than others. This was not of their own choosing but was marked out for them by God.

As we run this race, we must recognize that it is not a sprint but a marathon. So many young Christians start in a dead sprint, quickly burn out, and eventually quit. This was the case with those runners that had stopped halfway through their leg that night of the race. They grabbed the baton and sprinted up that hill without first counting the cost. Paul said, "Therefore I do not run like someone running aimlessly; I do not fight like a boxer beating the air" (1 Corinthians 9:26). We must discipline ourselves to run the race with patience so we don't burn out quickly but hard enough that we are satisfied when we cross that finish line that we gave it our all. As my old basketball coach used to say, play the game so that you leave everything on the court!

We must run with our eyes on the prize before us. When we have run a long, hard race, there is nothing sweeter than the site of the finish line in front of us. Paul said, "But one thing I do: Forgetting what is behind and straining toward what is ahead, I press on toward the goal to win the prize for which God has called me heavenward in Christ Jesus" (Philippians 3:13–14). No wonder I was elated when I came over that ridge and saw the lights of Las Vegas ahead! They were still a ways off, but what an encouragement to see the finish line in the distance.

As I look back over my life, I see many times when I ran hard and, unfortunately, a few times when I was caught loafing and not running as hard as I should have. But as Paul said, we are to forget what is behind us and strain toward what is ahead.

In my stage of life, I am much more focused on the finish line than I was at 35 when I was distracted by my career and family. But like Paul, my greatest desire is to finish strong. At the end of my life, I want to say with Paul as he was facing life's end, "I have fought the good fight, I have finished the race, I have kept the faith" (2 Timothy 4:7).

Father, help us identify the course You have laid out before us, and then give us the desire, discipline, strength, and stamina to run the race well. Forgive us when we get distracted and veer off course. May we always run with our sight on the prize You have set before us, and may we never take our eyes off you, the author and perfector of our faith. Lord, like Paul, give us the strength and determination to finish well. Amen.

Acknowledgments

First, I want to thank the Lord for blessing me with a career that has allowed me to see and experience so much. It is my prayer that the platform he has given me will in some way influence and encourage others in their walk.

To Jan, my lovely wife: You were always ready for a new adventure and never balked at the 11 moves to 8 different states throughout my 2 careers. Thank you for your selfless attitude and the wonderful mother you have been to our daughters.

To Jennifer, my eldest daughter: Thank you for helping me through this writing process as my content editor and advisor. Your ability to take a little "edge" off the writing of someone who often sees things as black and white has been invaluable.

To Rachel, my youngest daughter: Thank you for your loving encouragement through this journey. Your honesty, sense of humor, and matching wit have provided much material to write about in this book.

To Kyle, Jennifer, Nick, and Rachel: Thank you for being the godly parents you are to our grandchildren. No father could be prouder of the way you are bringing up your kids in the gentle training and instruction of the Lord.

To Harper, Reagan, Hutton, Mason, Ryder, and Blakely: You grandchildren are the original inspiration for this book. I pray that you will eventually fully appreciate the godly legacy passed down in our family from generation to generation.

To Donna Lee Toney: Thanks for all the writing tips and for taking the time to read over the initial chapters. Your editorial comments were such a help.

To Dr. Bill Heston, friend and mentor: Your encouragement to continue and feedback on the manuscript will always be remembered and appreciated.

To my Lucid Books publishing family: Thank you for the guidance and expertise you gave me as a novice writer through this process. I'm not sure it would have ever become a reality without your help.

Notes

1. Mother Teresa, "National Prayer Breakfast Speech," n.d., https://www.americanrhetoric.com/speeches/motherteresanationalprayerbreakfast.htm.
2. Mother Teresa, "National Prayer Breakfast Speech."
3. Mother Teresa, "National Prayer Breakfast Speech."
4. Mother Teresa, "National Prayer Breakfast Speech."
5. "Remembering Guyana's 1992 Elections, an Excerpt from 'Beyond the White House,' by Jimmy Carter," The Carter Center, n.d., https://www.cartercenter.org/news/features/p/democracy/remembering-guyanna-1992-elections.html.
6. David O'Reilly, "When You Say You Believe In God, What Do You Mean?," The Pew Charitable Trusts, November 2, 2018, https://www.pewtrusts.org/en/trust/archive/fall-2018/when-you-say-you-believe-in-god-what-do-you-mean.
7. Benjamin Fearnow, "52 Percent of Americans Say Jesus Isn't God but Was a Great Teacher, Survey Says," Newsweek, August 30, 2020, https://www.newsweek.com/52-percent-americans-say-jesus-isnt-not-god-was-great-teacher-survey-says-1528617.
8. "Oprah Says There Are Many Ways to God- What a Shame - Popular Christian Videos," Video, GodTube, n.d., https://www.godtube.com/watch/?v=GYGLWNNX.
9. Mark Banschick M.D., "Regret-8 Ways to Move On," Psychology Today.com, May 1, 2015, accessed October 1, 2022, https://www.psychologytoday.com/us/blog/the-intelligent-divorce/201505/regret-8-ways-move.
10. American Experience, "Alzheimer's Letter," American Experience | PBS, March 13, 2019, https://www.pbs.org/wgbh/americanexperience/features/reagan-alzheimers/.
11. EveryHomeUSA, "Testimony | Jim Cymbala," Video, YouTube, February 8, 2018, https://www.youtube.com/watch?v=zxE0wAl2-dg
12. "You've Got to Find What You Love, Jobs Says," Stanford News, August 24, 2022, https://news.stanford.edu/2005/06/12/youve-got-find-love-jobs-says/.
13. Darian Lusk, "Elvis Turns 80: 10 Fascinating Facts about The King," CBS News, January 10, 2015, https://www.cbsnews.com/news/elvis-80th-birthday-10-fascinating-facts-about-elvis-presley/.
14. Juliana Menasce Horowitz and Nikki Graf, "Most U.S. Teens See Anxiety and Depression as a Major Problem Among Their Peers," Pew Research Center's Social

& Demographic Trends Project, May 30, 2020, https://www.pewresearch.org/social-trends/2019/02/20/most-u-s-teens-see-anxiety-and-depression-as-a-major-problem-among-their-peers/.

15. Tracy Briggs, "The Anxious Generation: Why Young People Are Lonely and Stressed," West Central Tribune, January 7, 2020, https://www.wctrib.com/lifestyle/the-anxious-generation-why-young-people-are-lonely-and-stressed.

16. Don Joseph Goewey, "85 Percent of What We Worry About Never Happens," HuffPost, December 7, 2017, https://www.huffpost.com/entry/85-of-what-we-worry-about_b_8028368.

17. Cambridge Dictionary: Access Online: Viewed 4/2023: https://dictionary.cambridge.org/us/.

18. Reasons for Hope* Jesus, "George HW Bush Inaugural Prayer," Video, YouTube, August 10, 2016, https://www.youtube.com/watch?v=FTIWwLtmCfM.